Abuja metropolis might be one of the biggest and fastest growing cities in Africa, known to be the federal capital of **Nigeria** (the GIANT of Africa) and notable for its remarkable neatness and beautiful landscapes and edifices in the metropolis, it attracts increasing influx of settlers from other neighboring states within the country searching for greener pastures and better standard of living.

But it is quite ironically interesting that majority of the population estimated in the year 2015 to be over 3,000,000 million can not afford to live in Abuja metropolis because the cost of accommodation is disarming.

The estimated amount for one year rent on an apartment in Wuse, Maitama, Gwarimpa, Garki, (all districts in Abuja metropolis) could gobble up an entire year's income leaving nothing for other expenses: for this reasons most settlers would rather live in the outskirts of town and smaller settlements in Karu, Kubwa, Lugbe, Nyanya, Mpape, Dutse, Bwari, Gishiri: these locations may not be as neat, extravagant and beautiful as the districts but they are livable.

Offices, government agencies, federal ministries, private establishments and most established business are sited in the metropolis, now people live in the outskirt of town but commute to work every morning 5 days of the week. And on weekends what happens to the beautiful metropolis of Abuja? Its hustle and bustle ends on Friday night after a successful work week and on weekends its really deserted and void of much excitement with not much of activity happening…. Welcome to Lazy Weekend in Abuja!!!

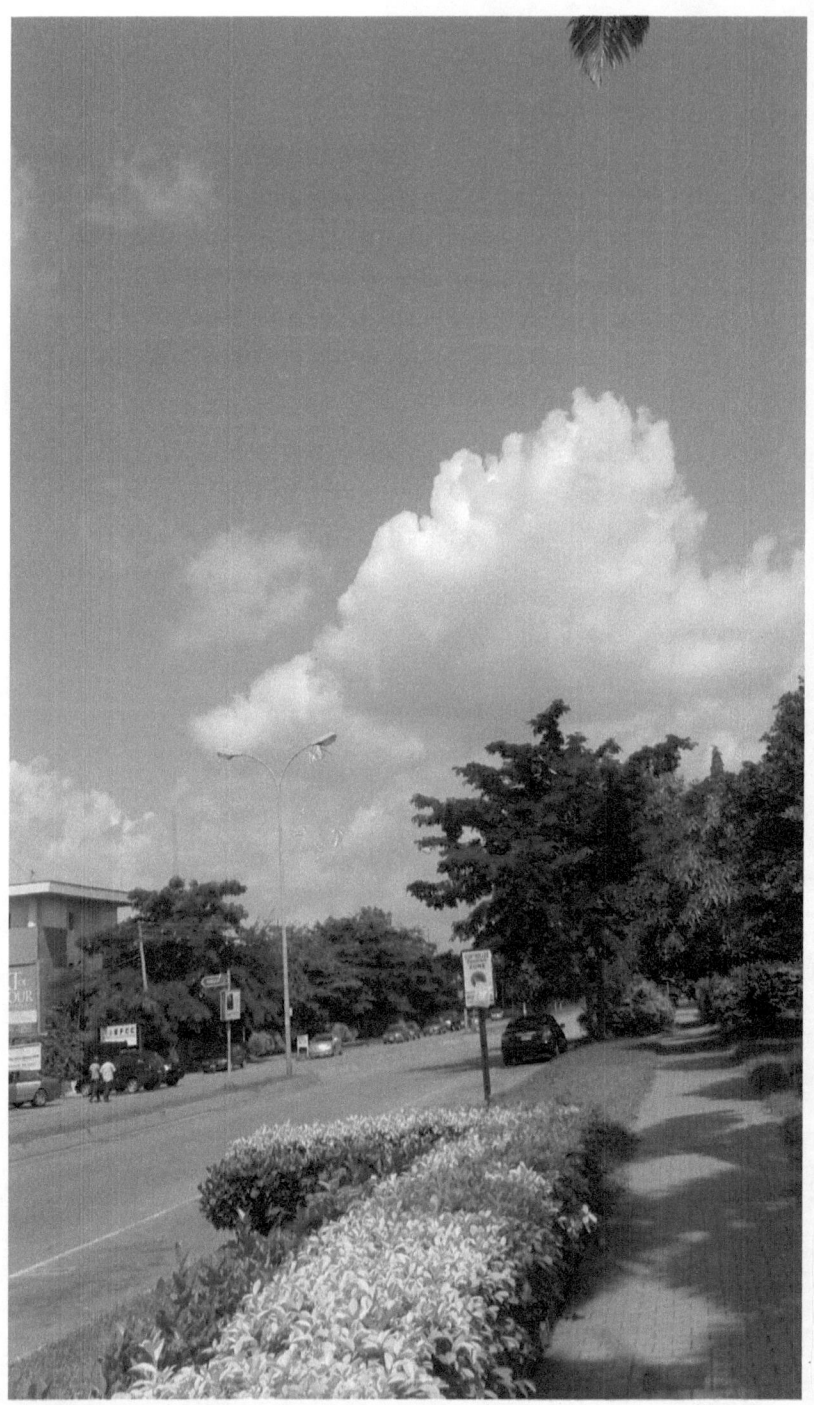

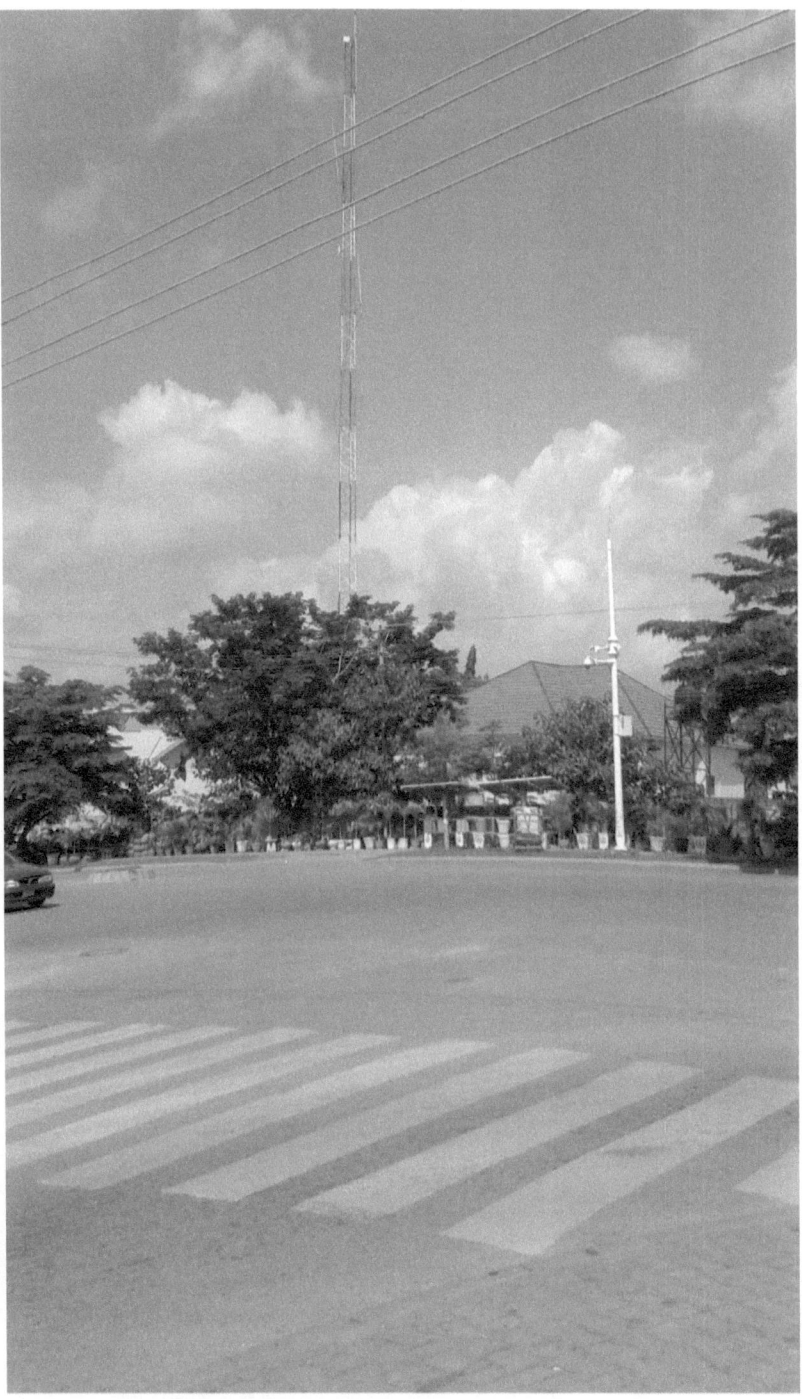

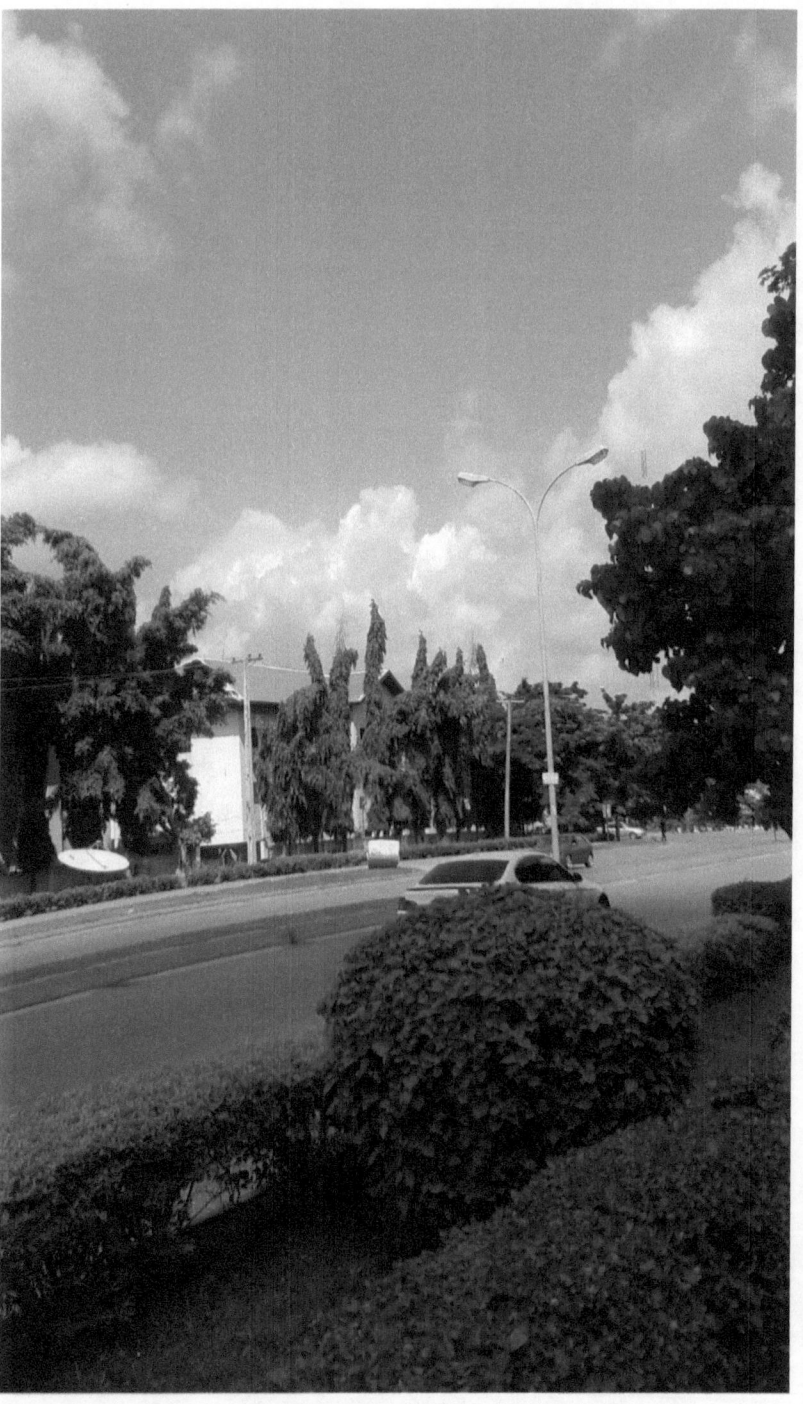

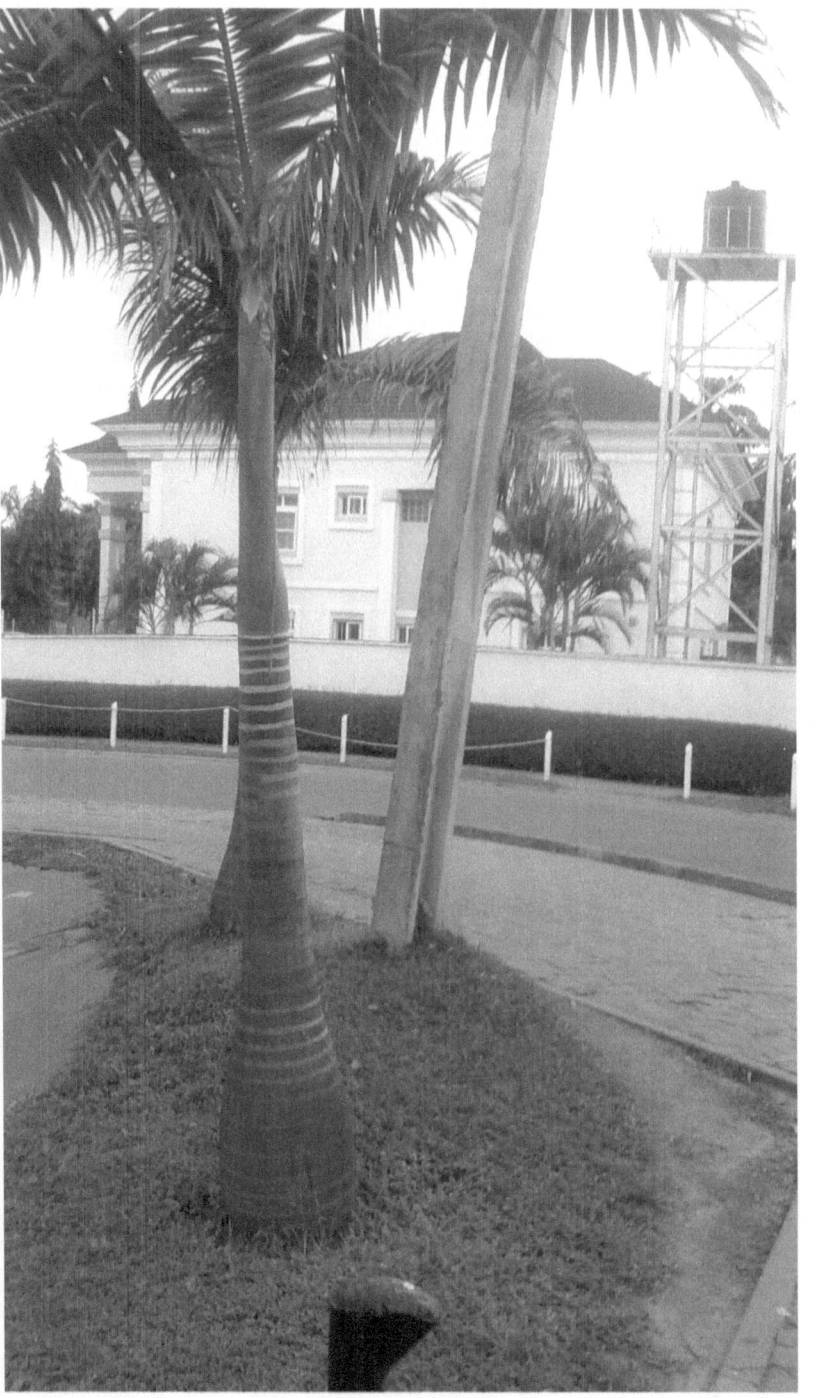

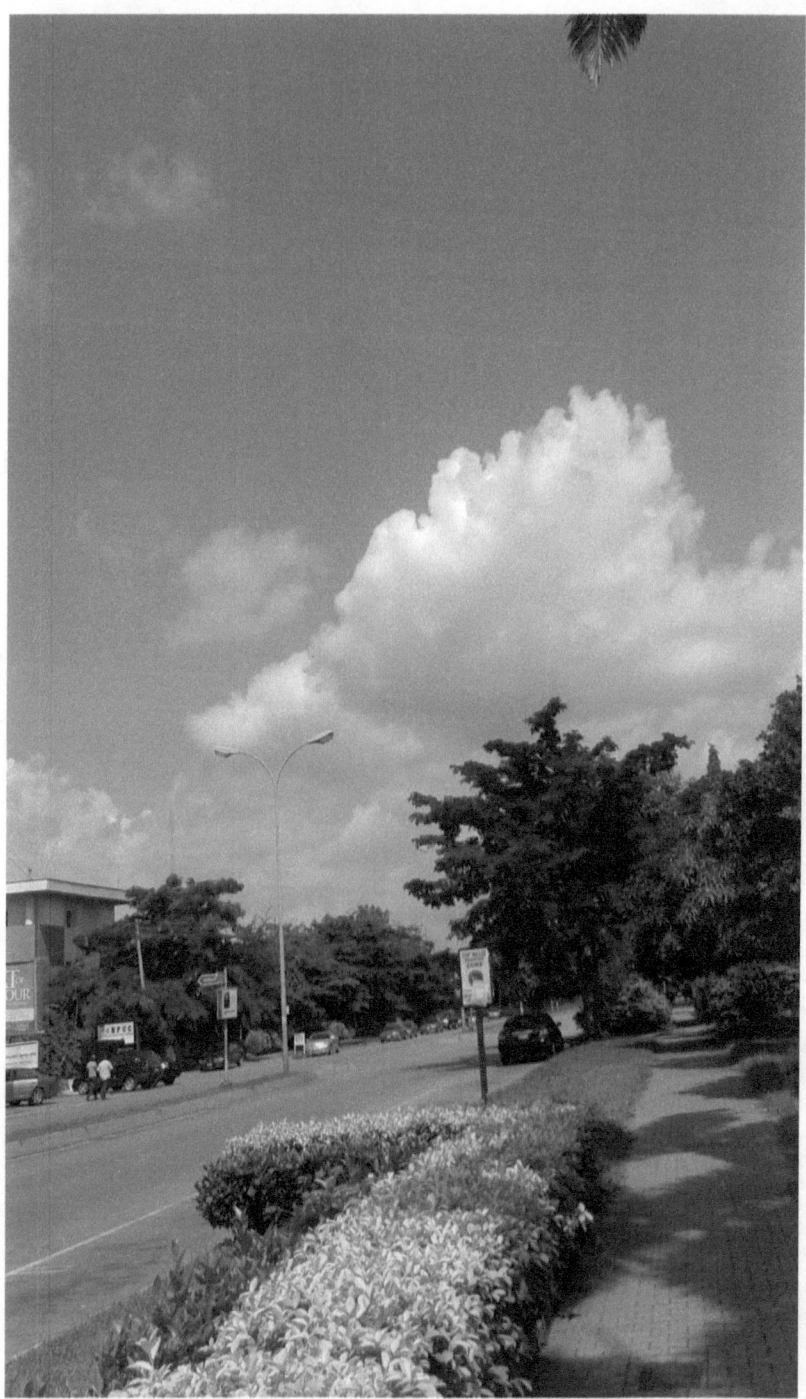

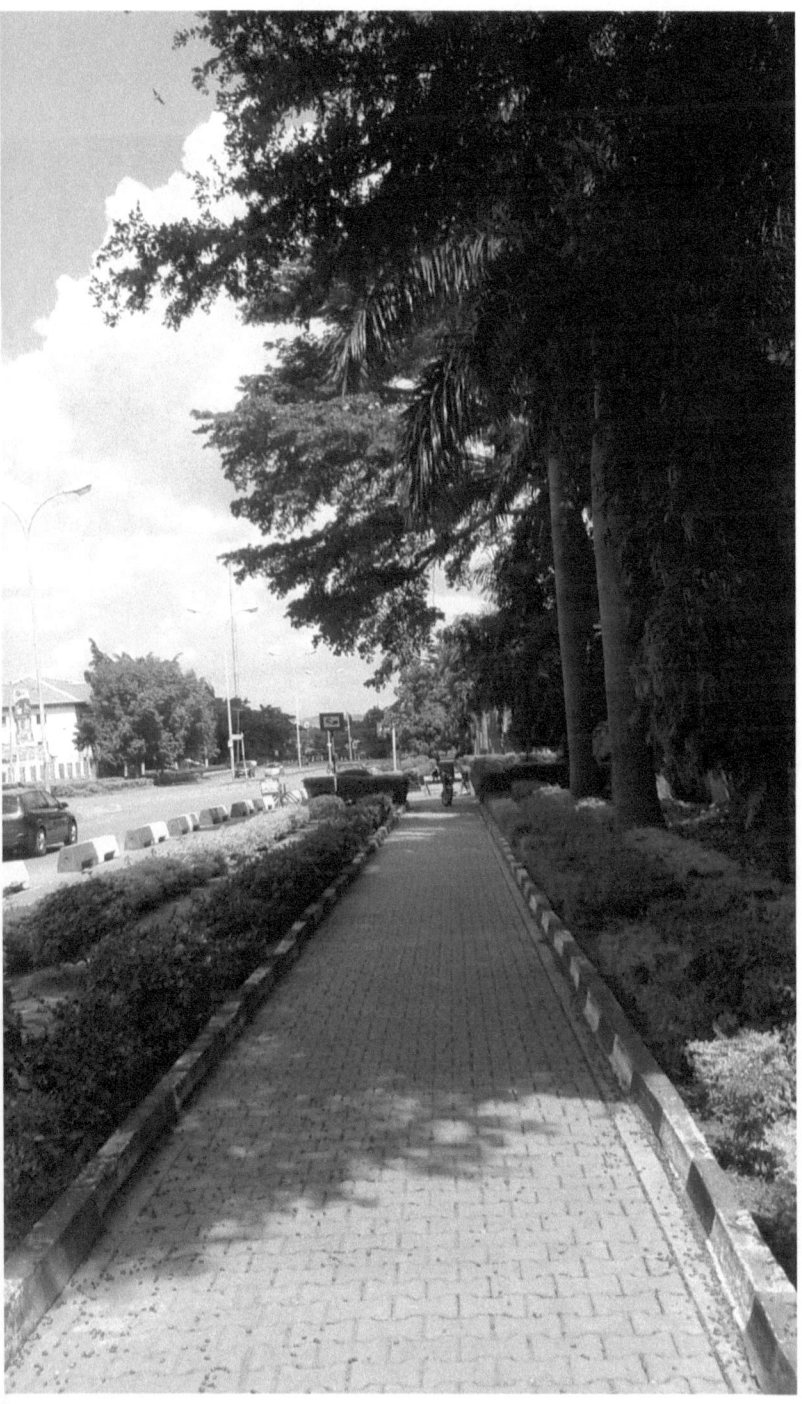

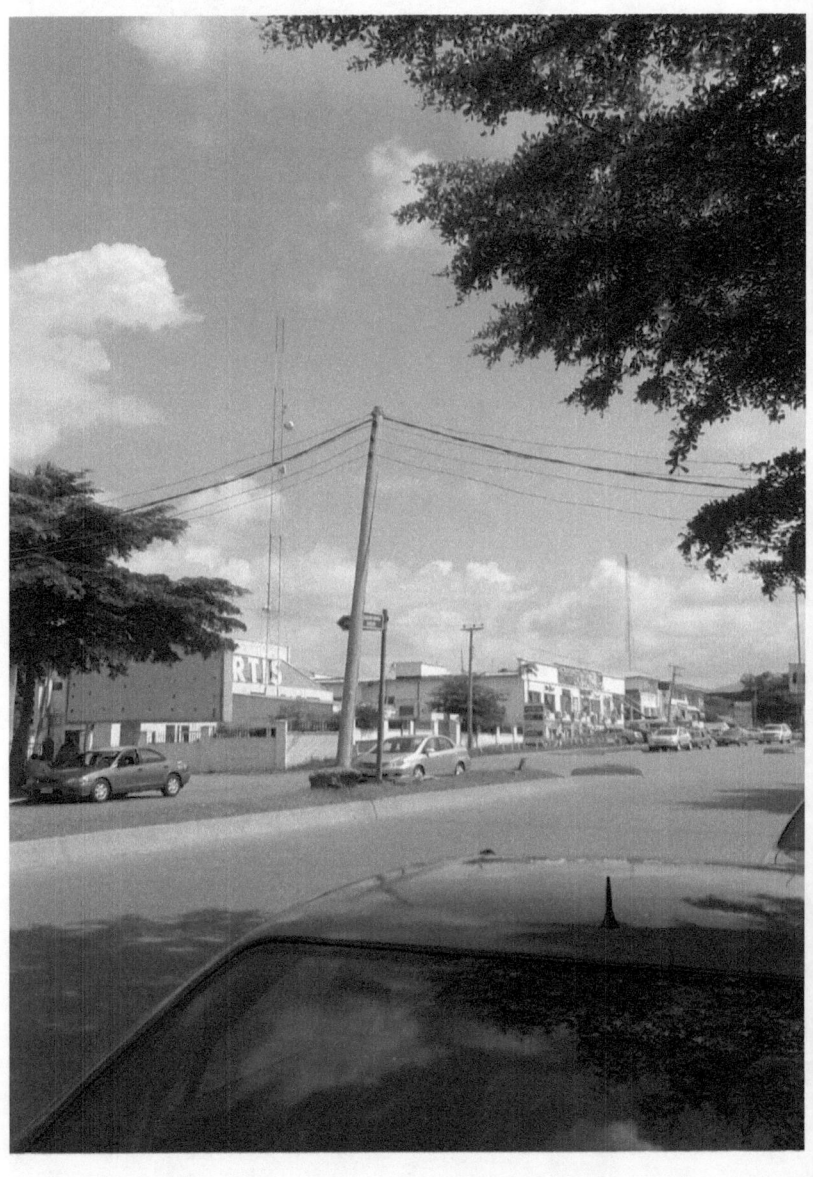

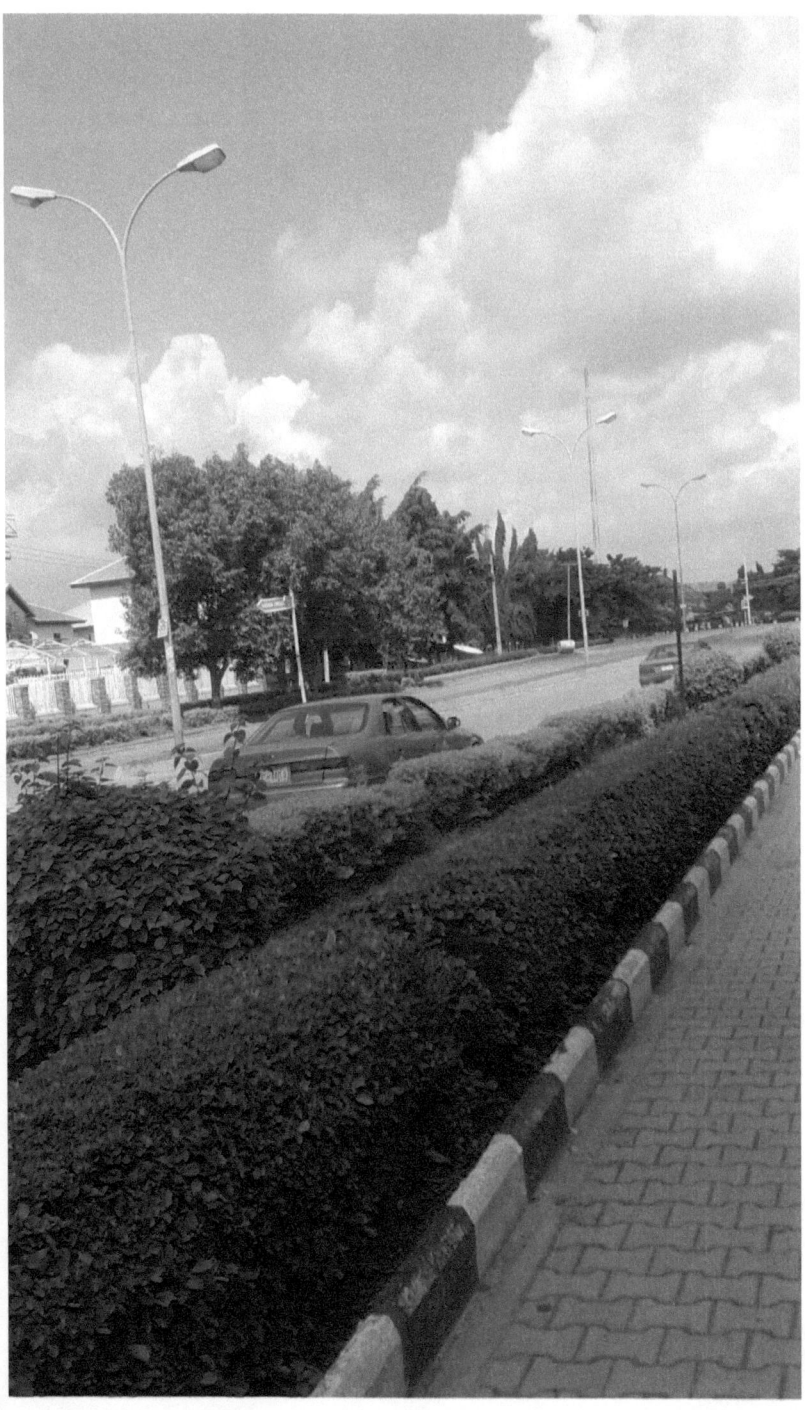

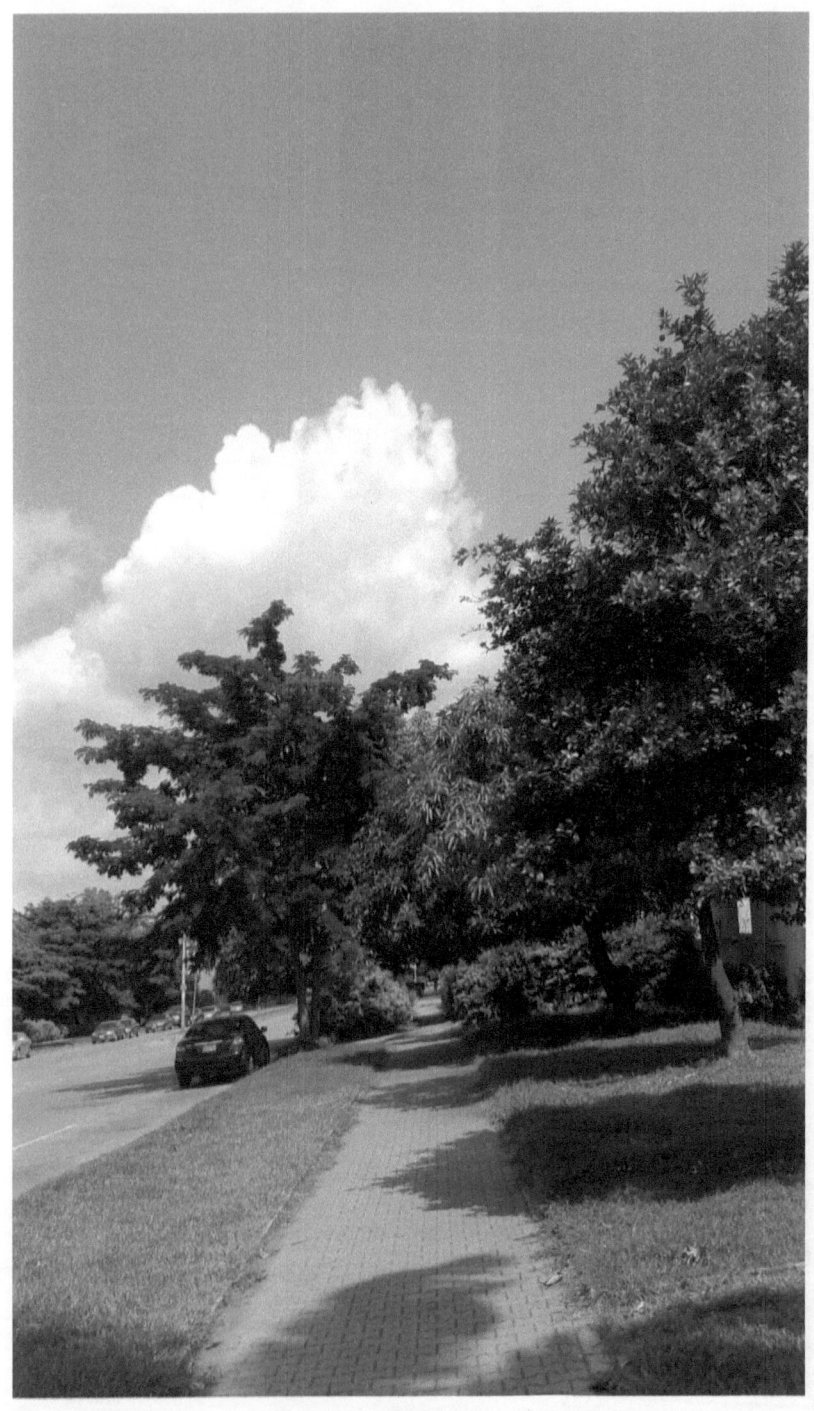

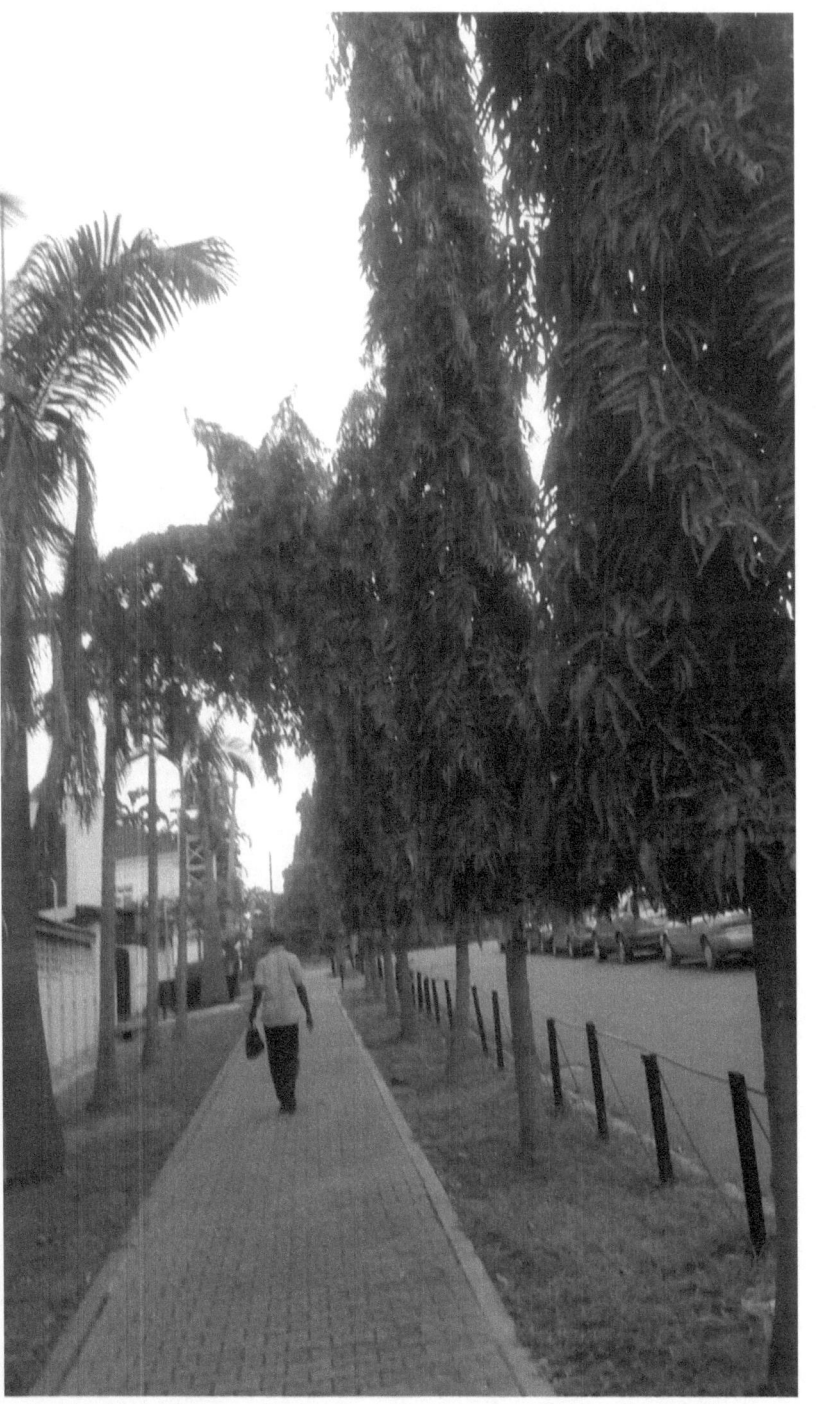

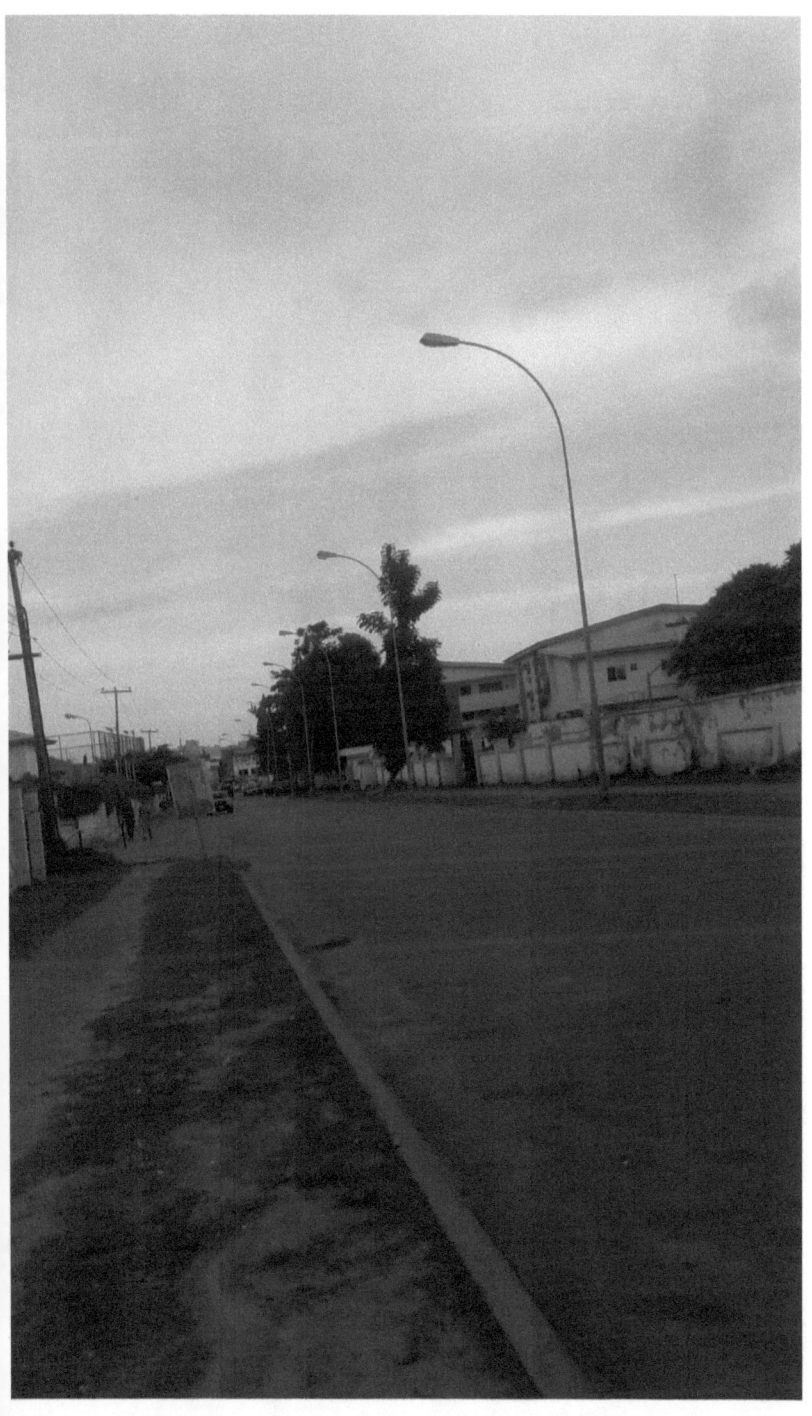

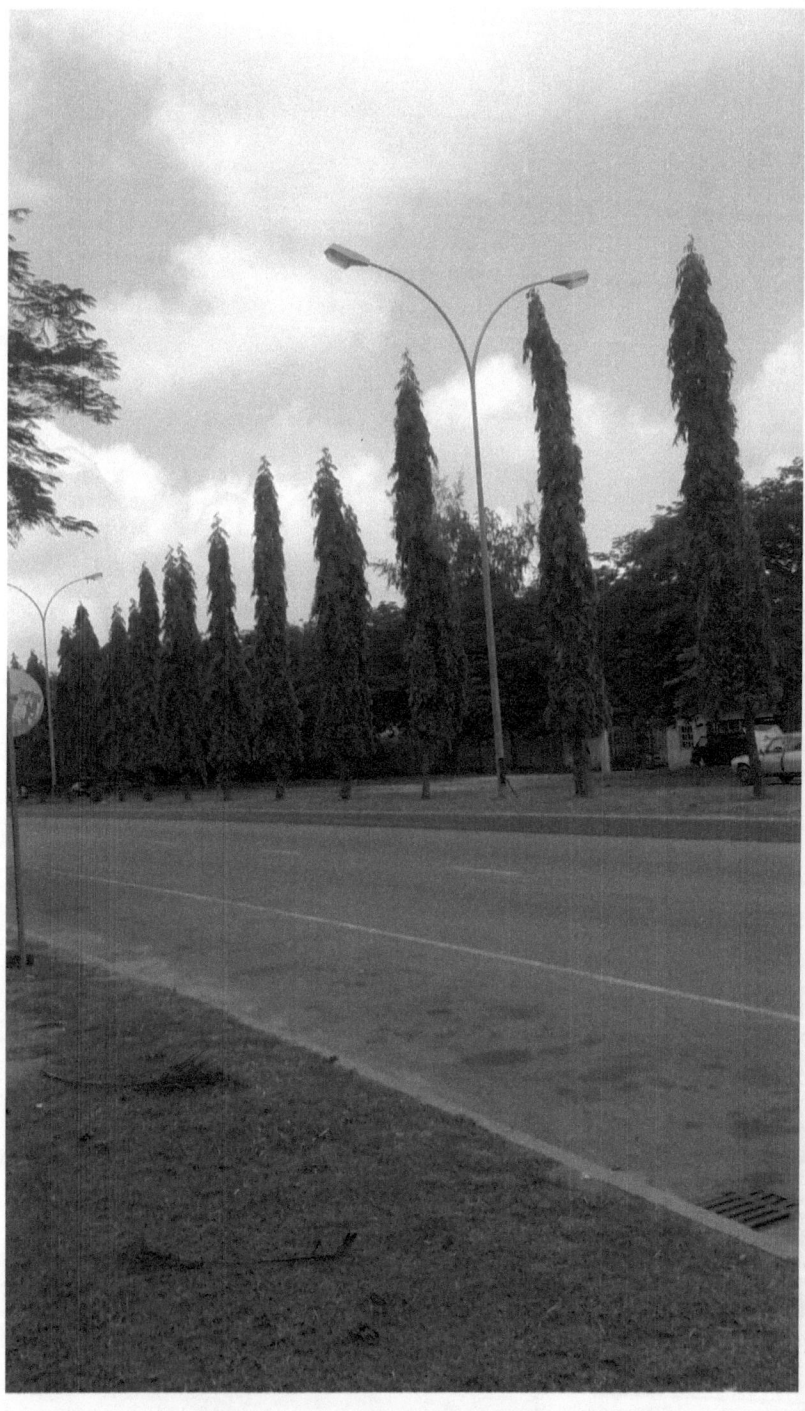

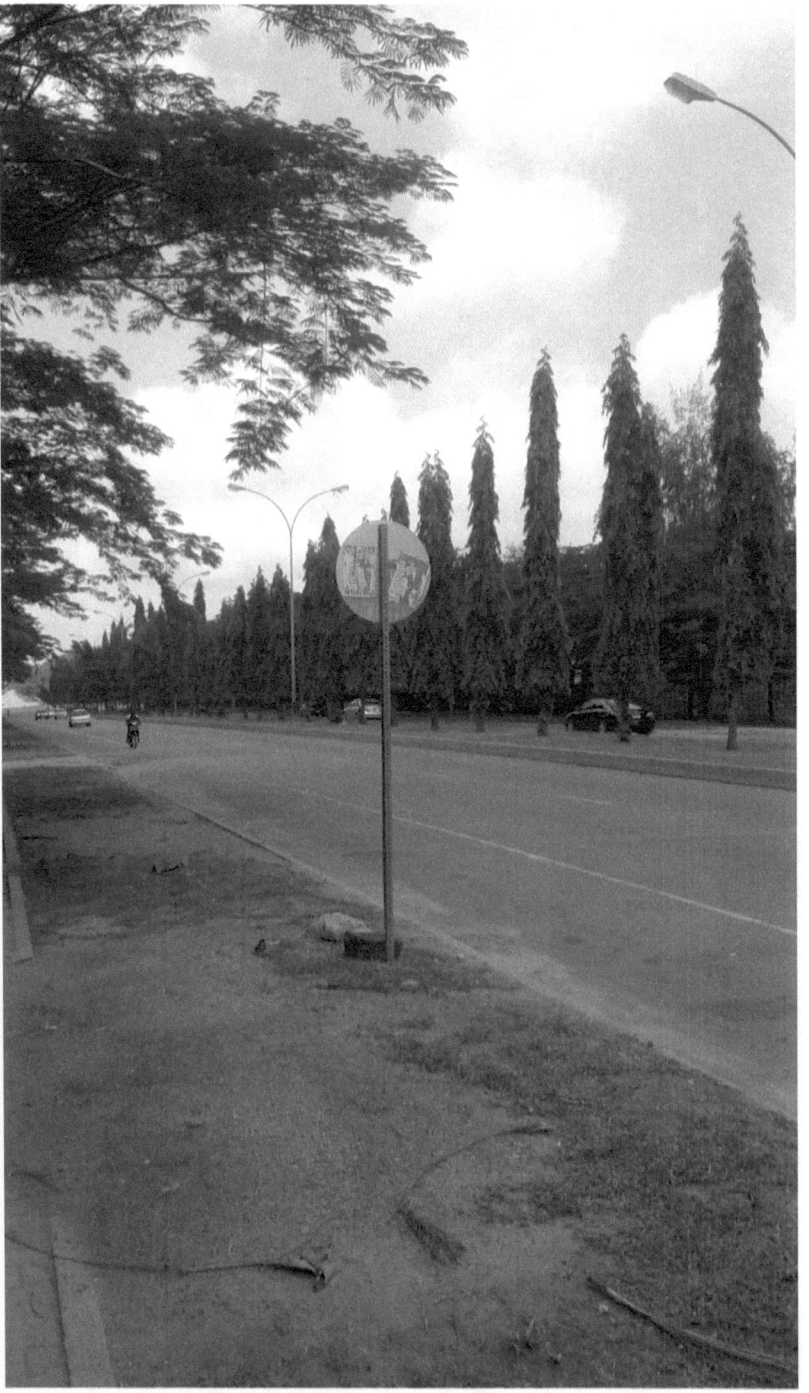

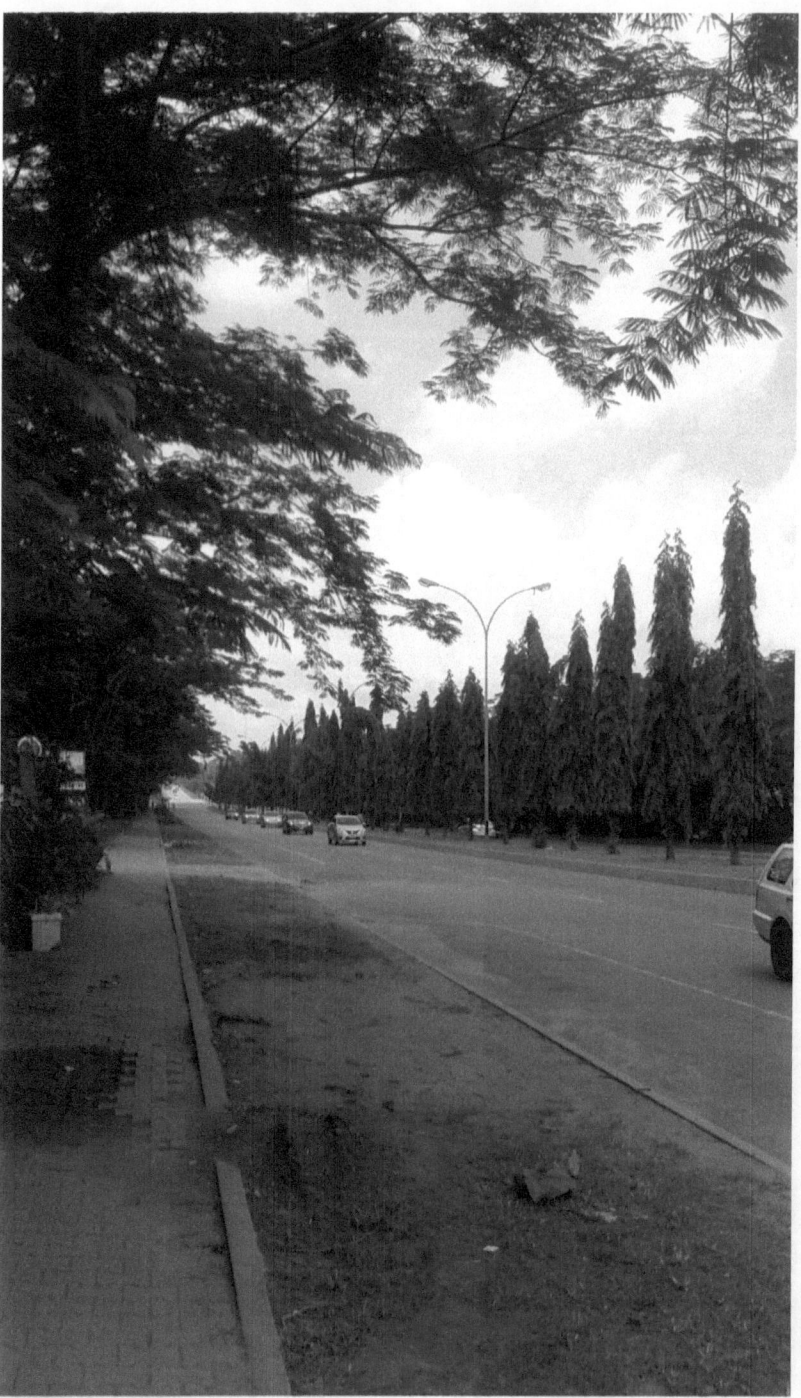

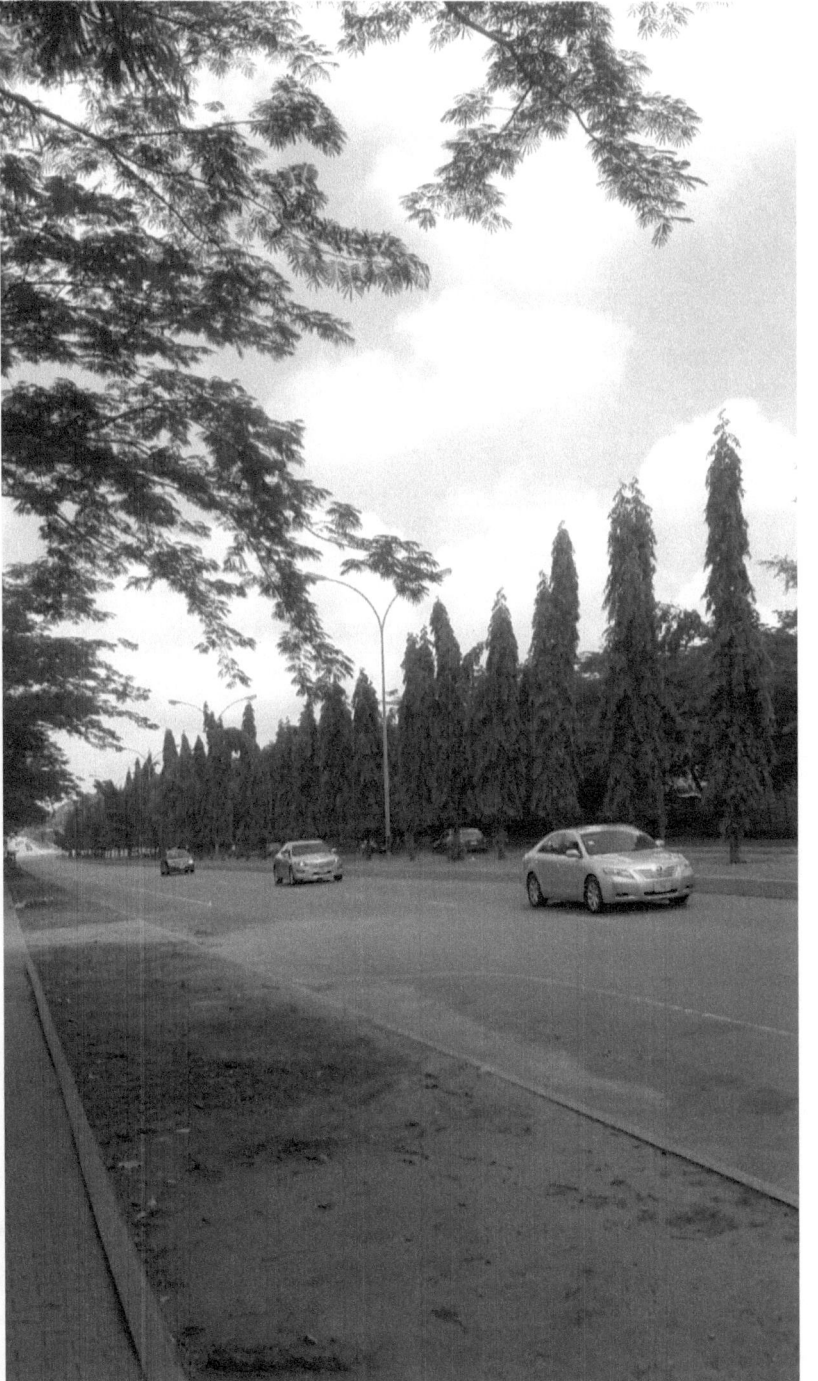

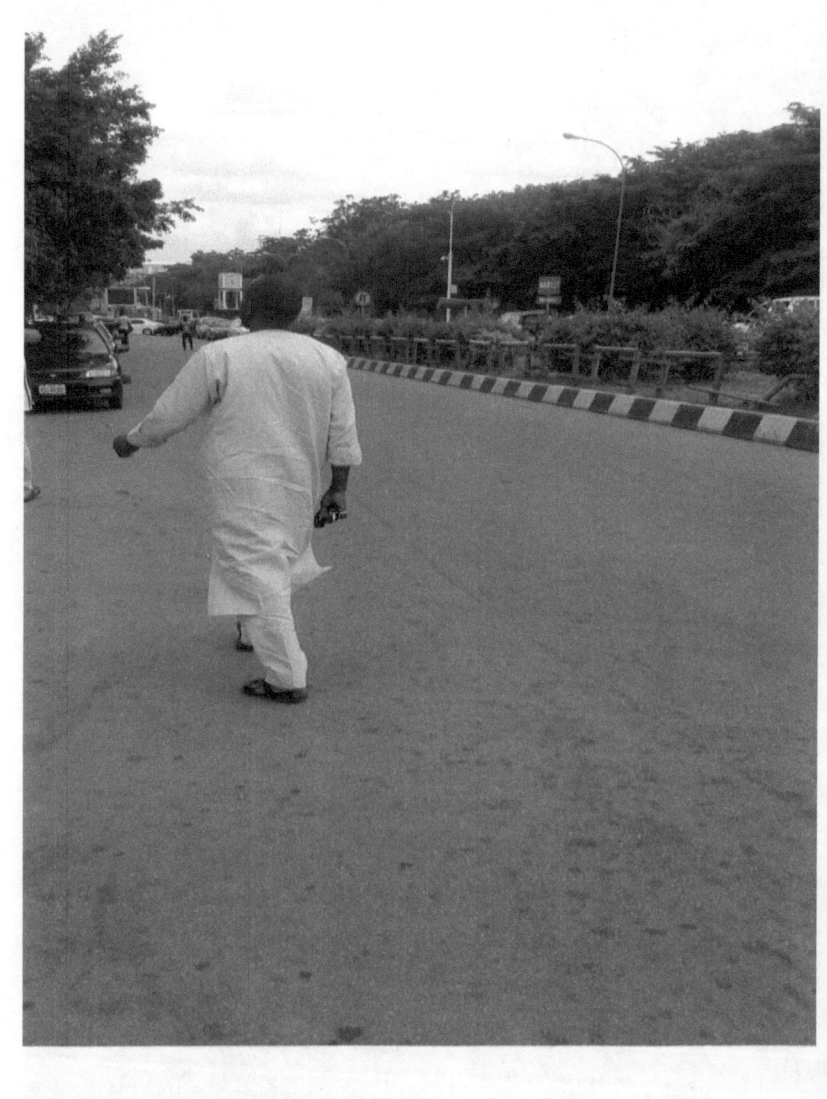

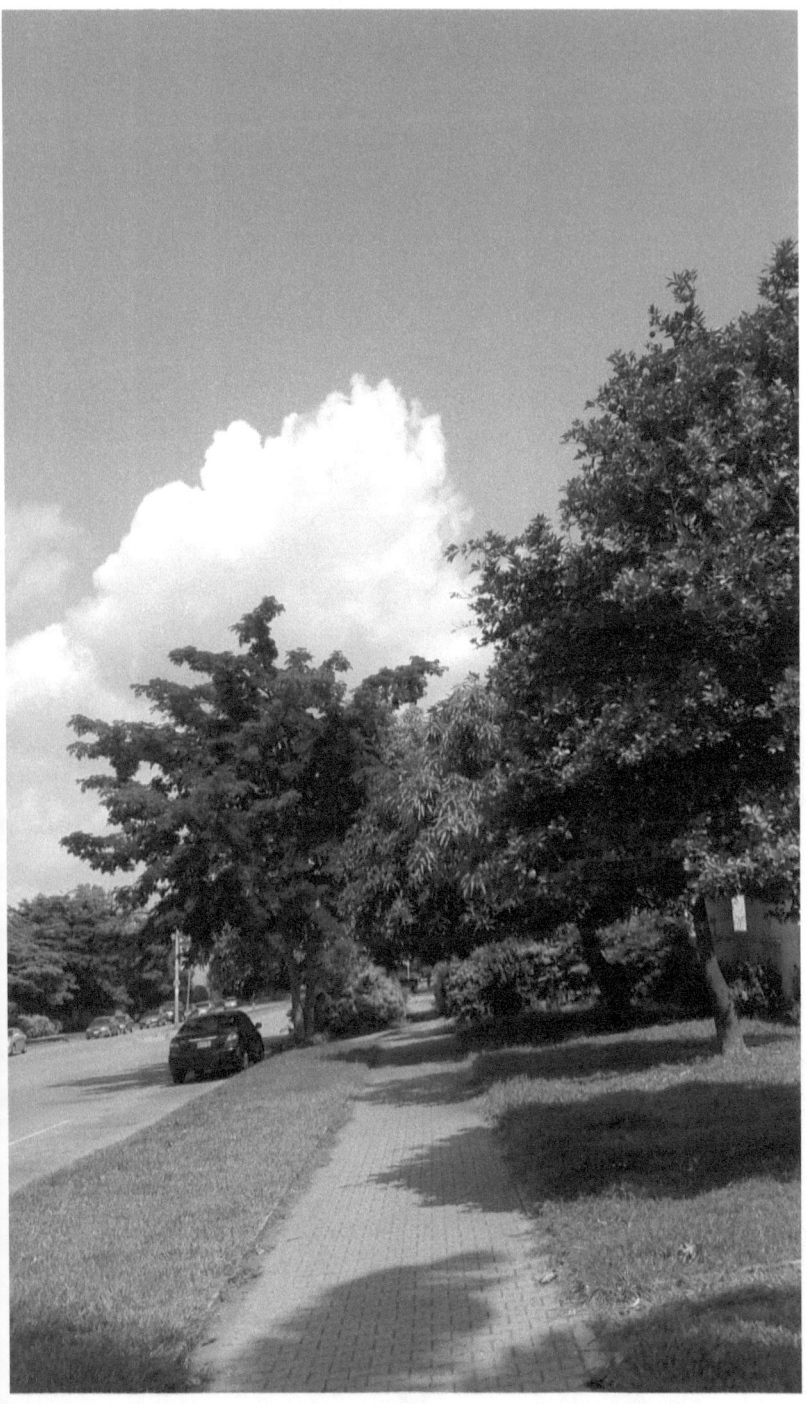

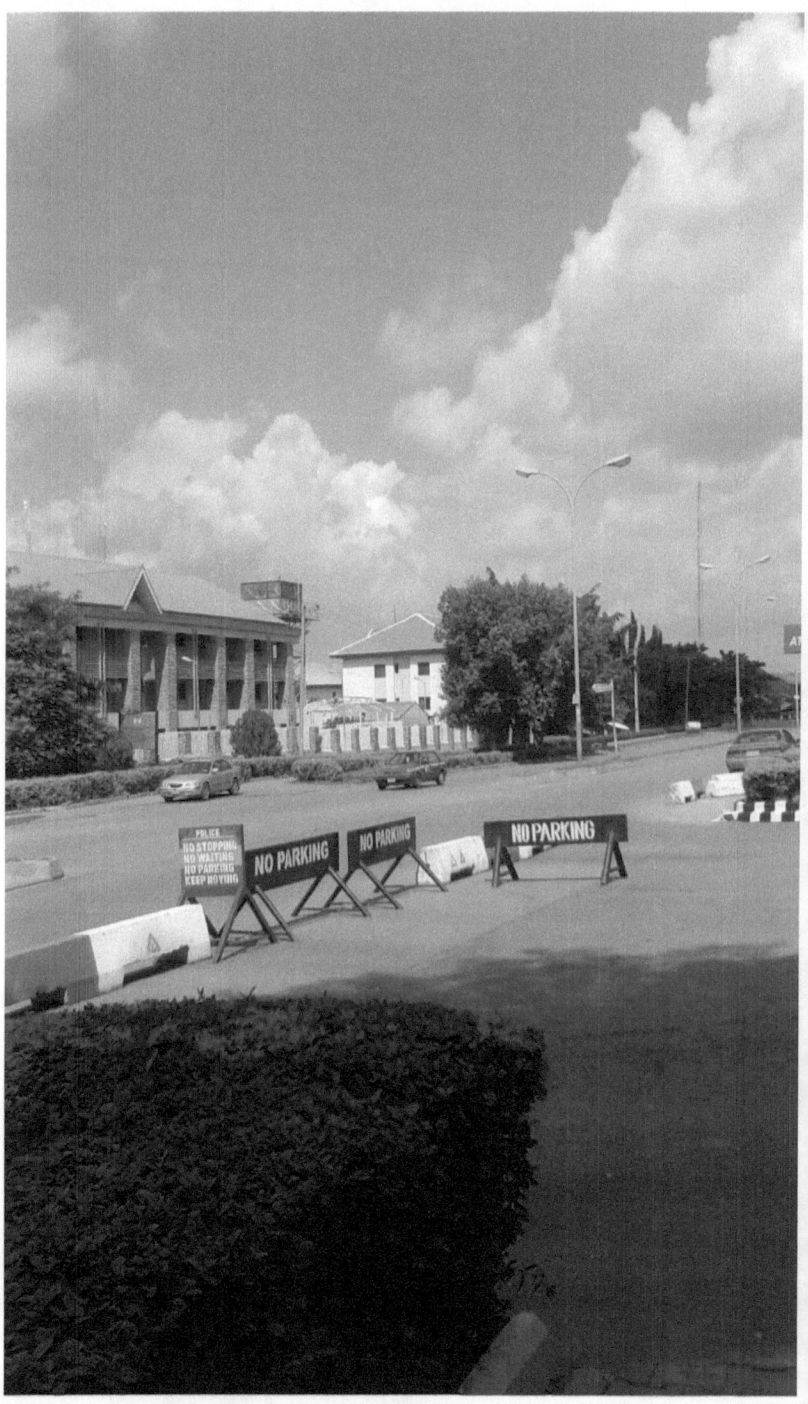

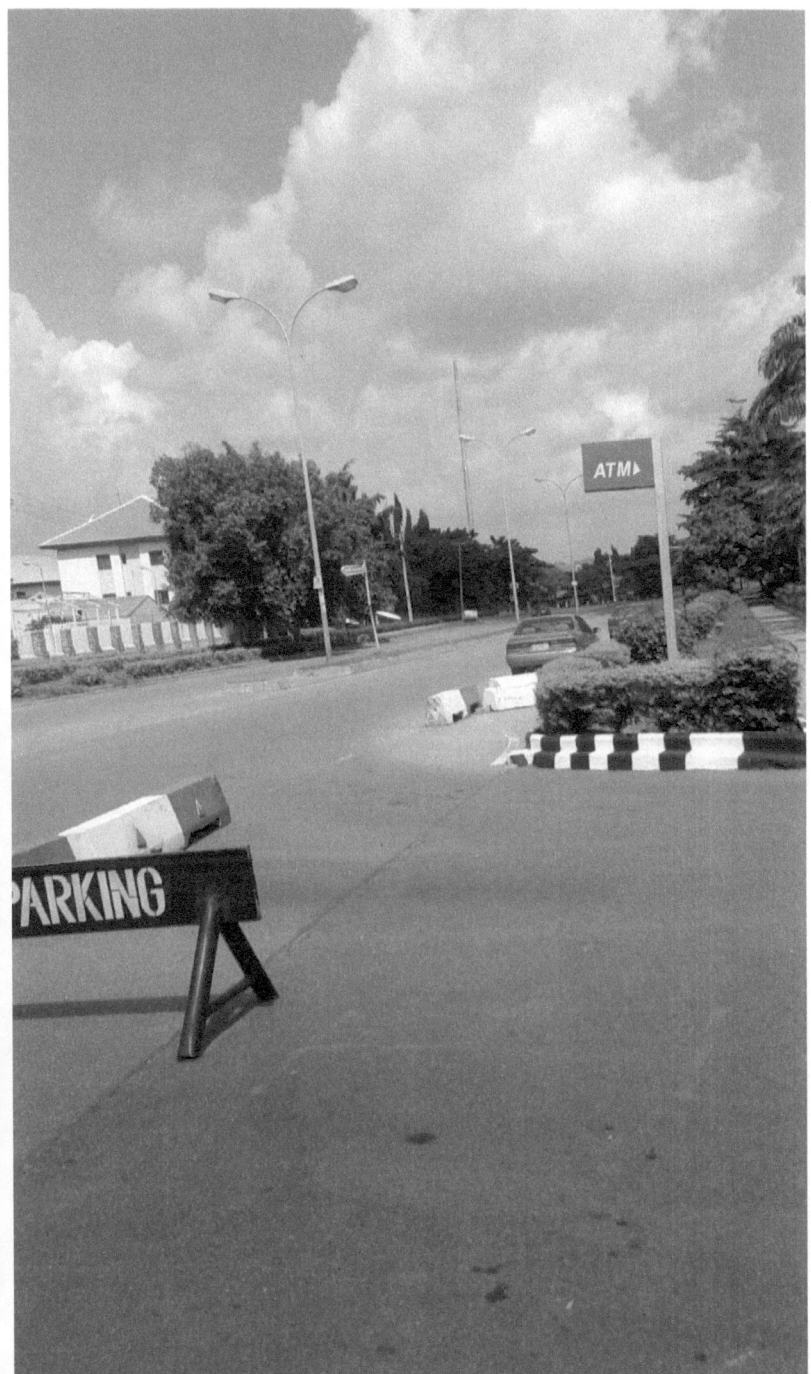

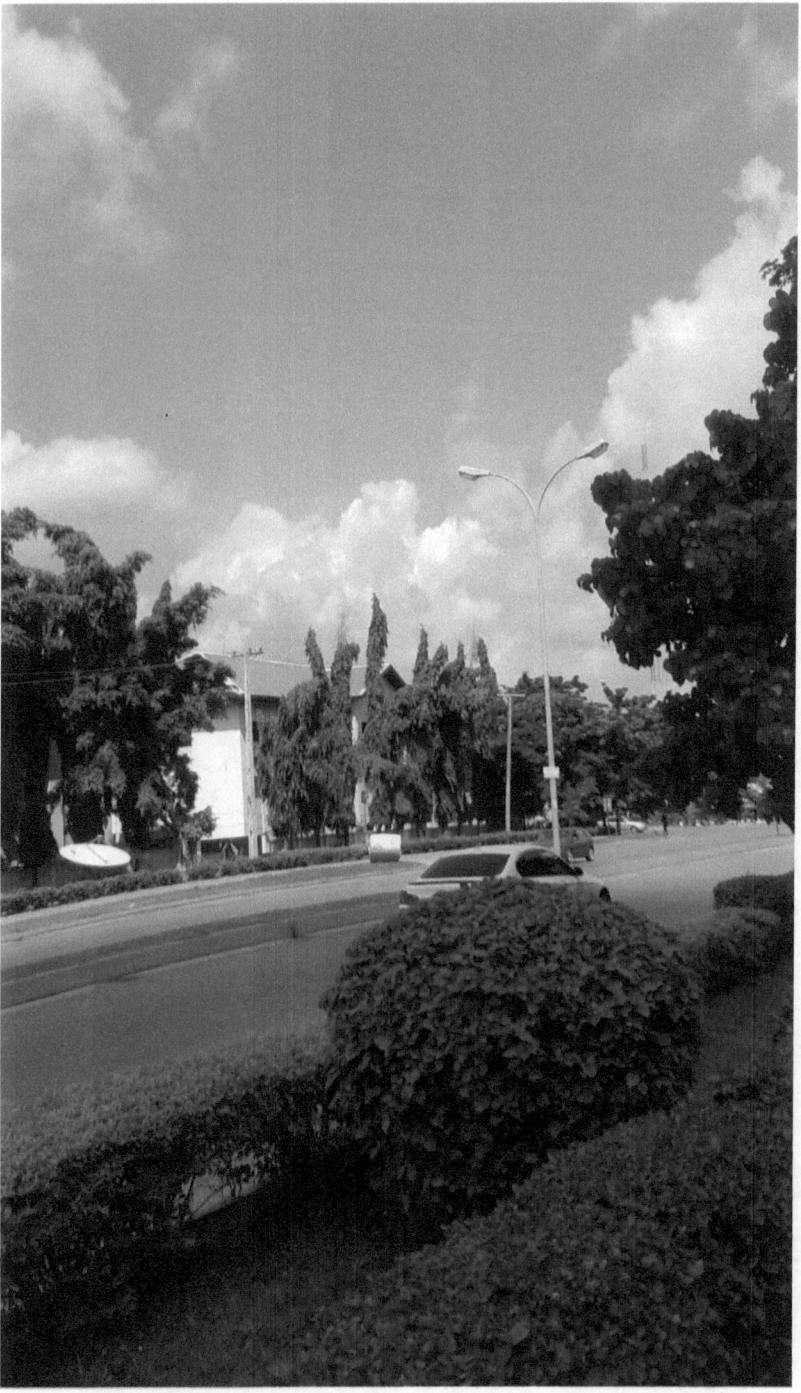

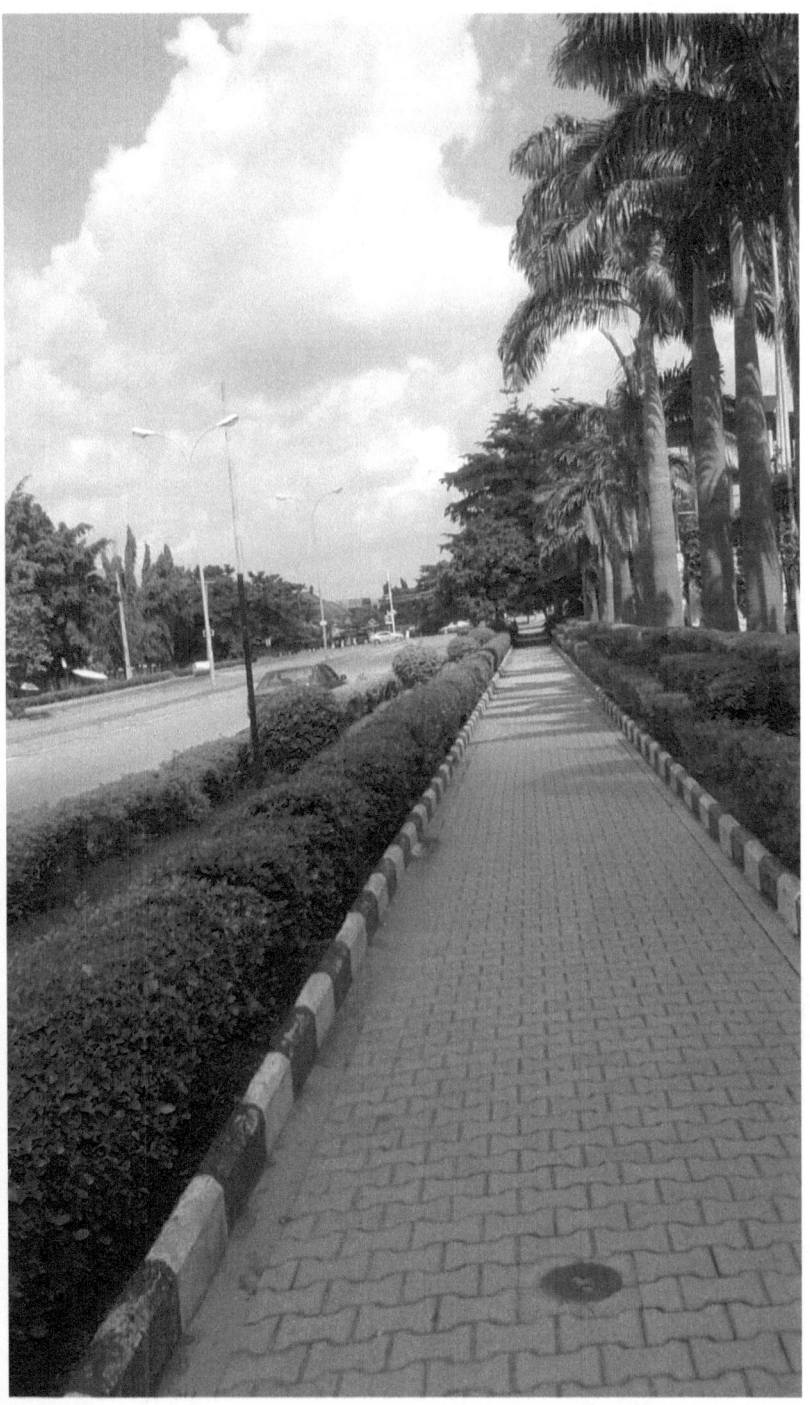

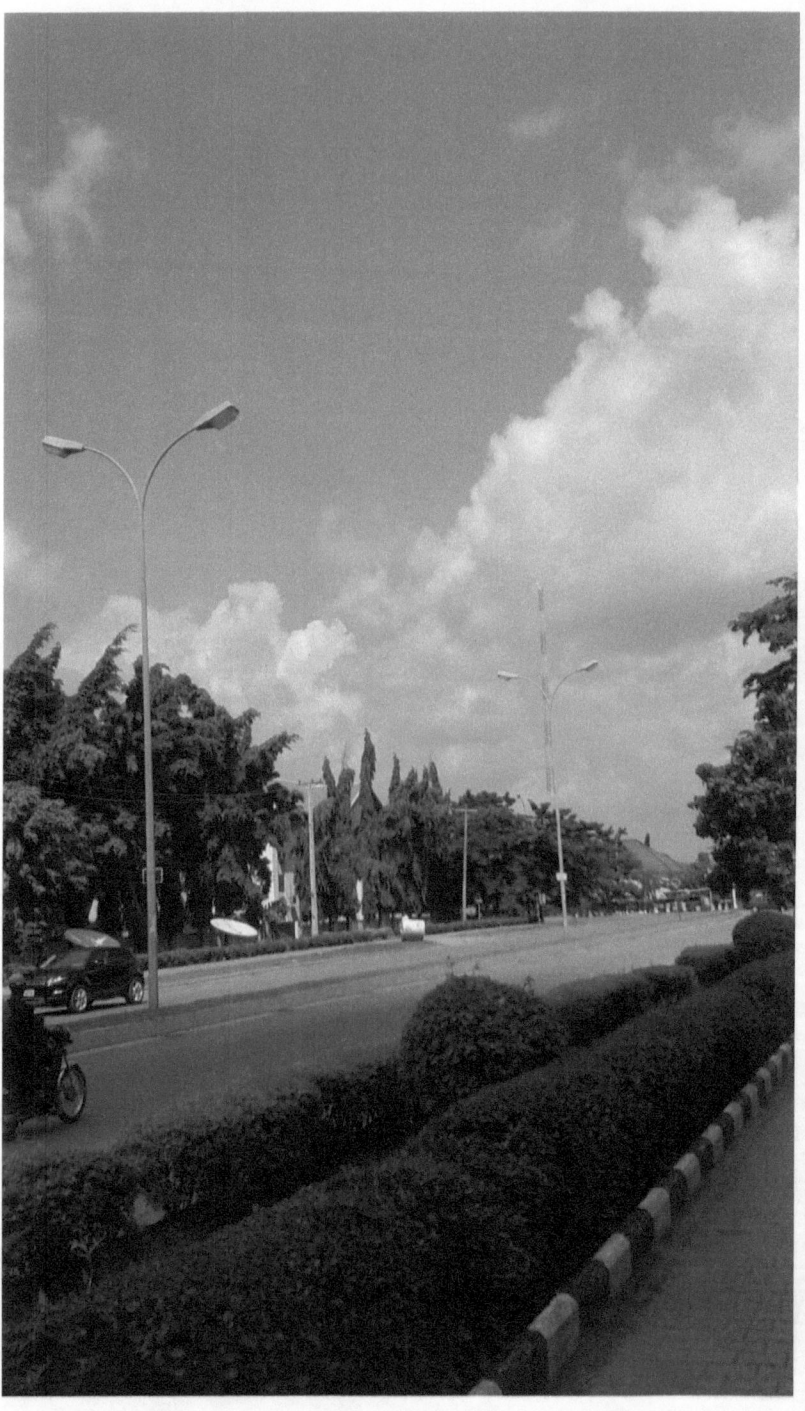

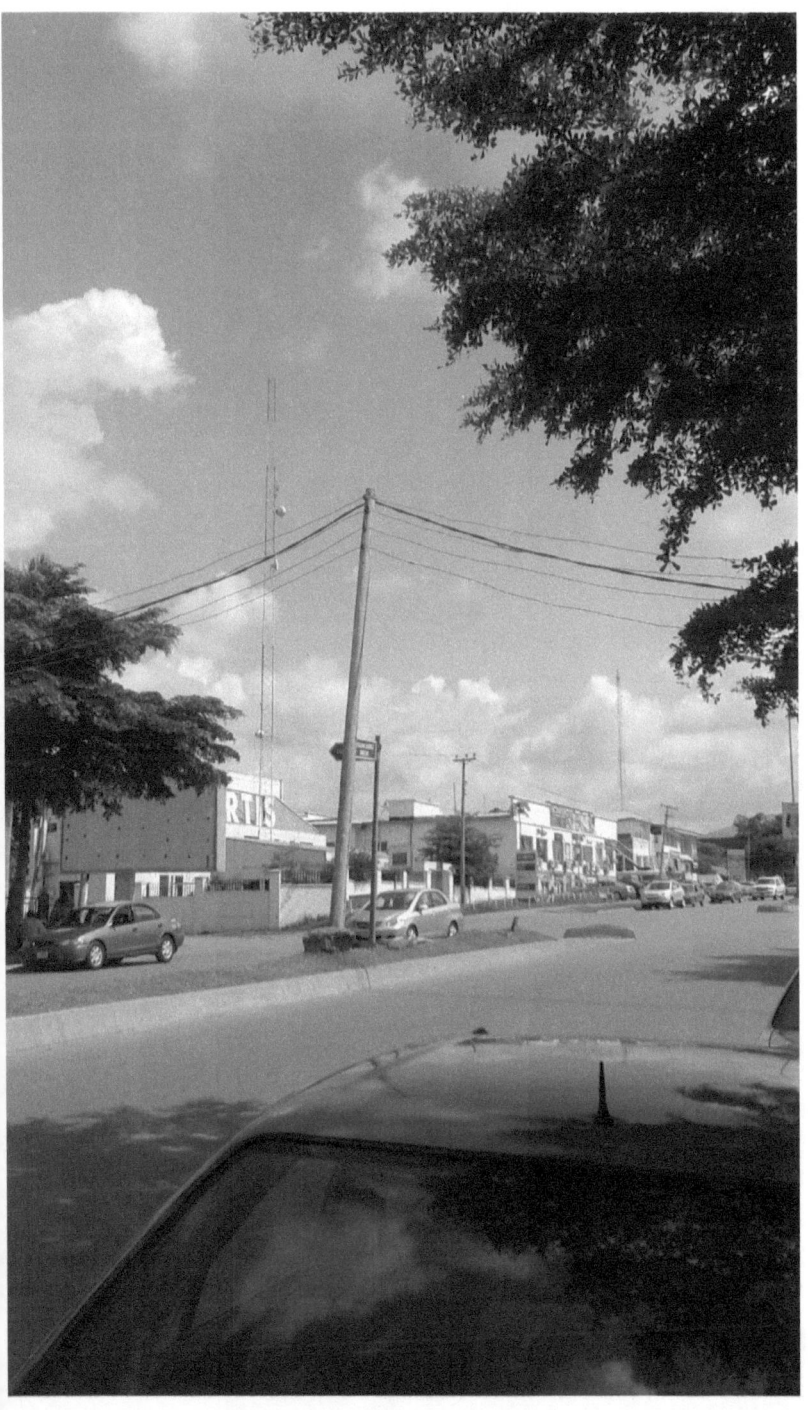

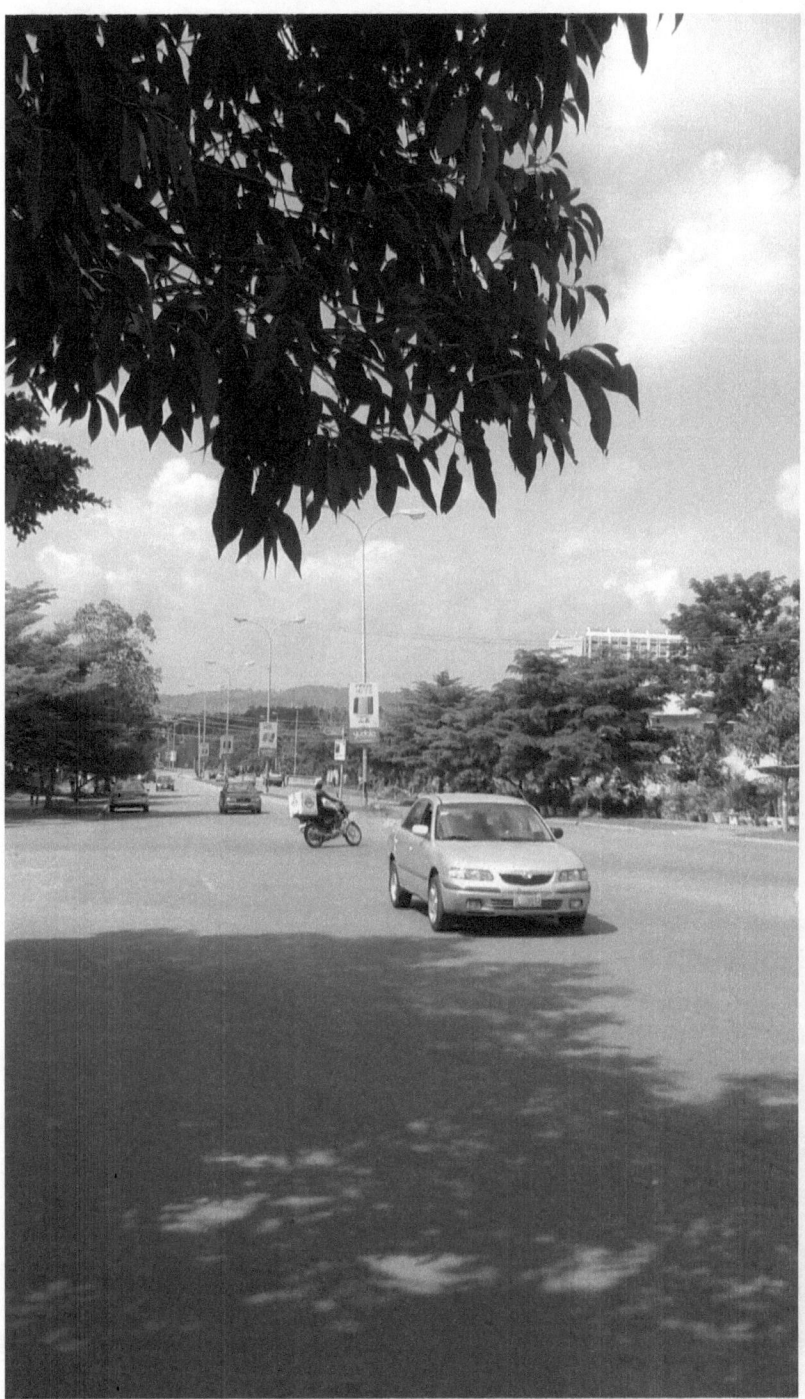

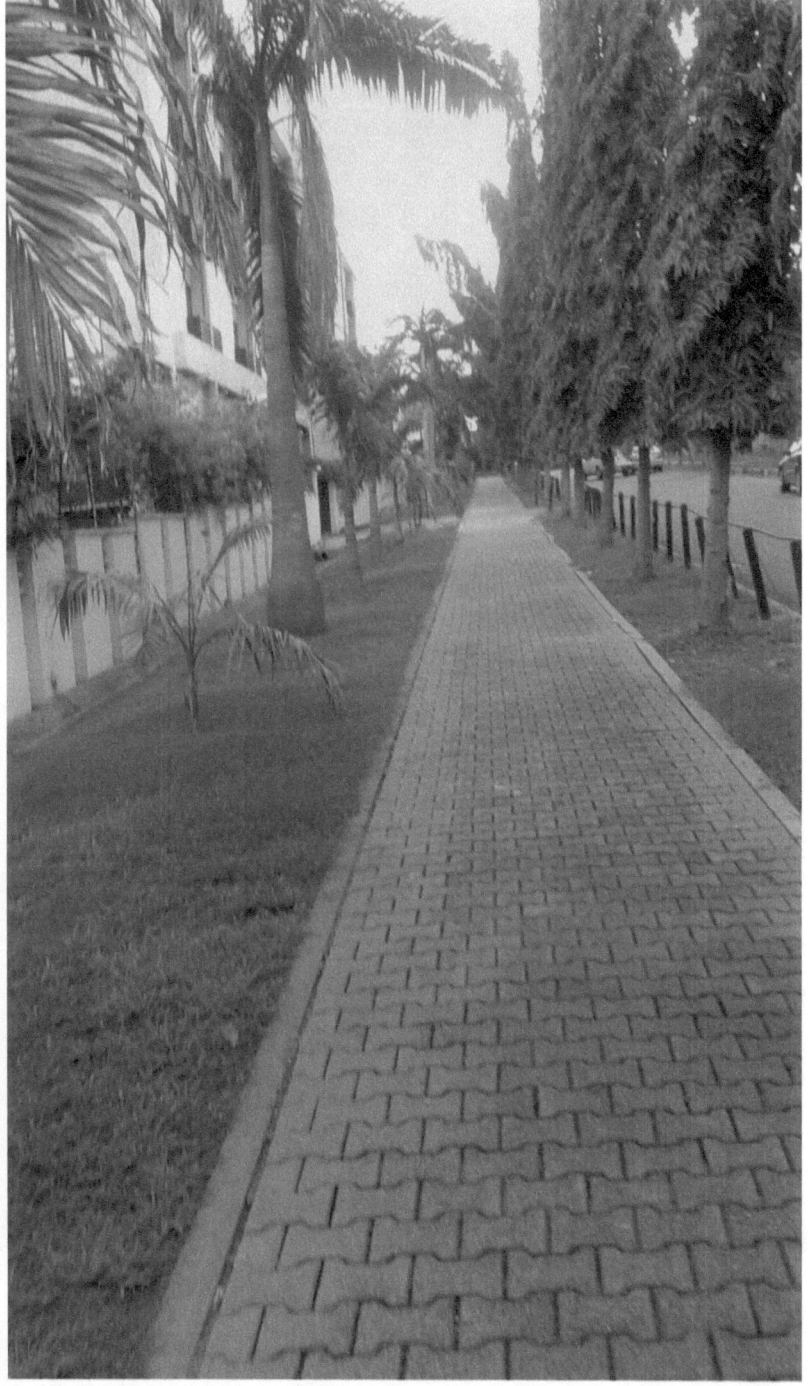

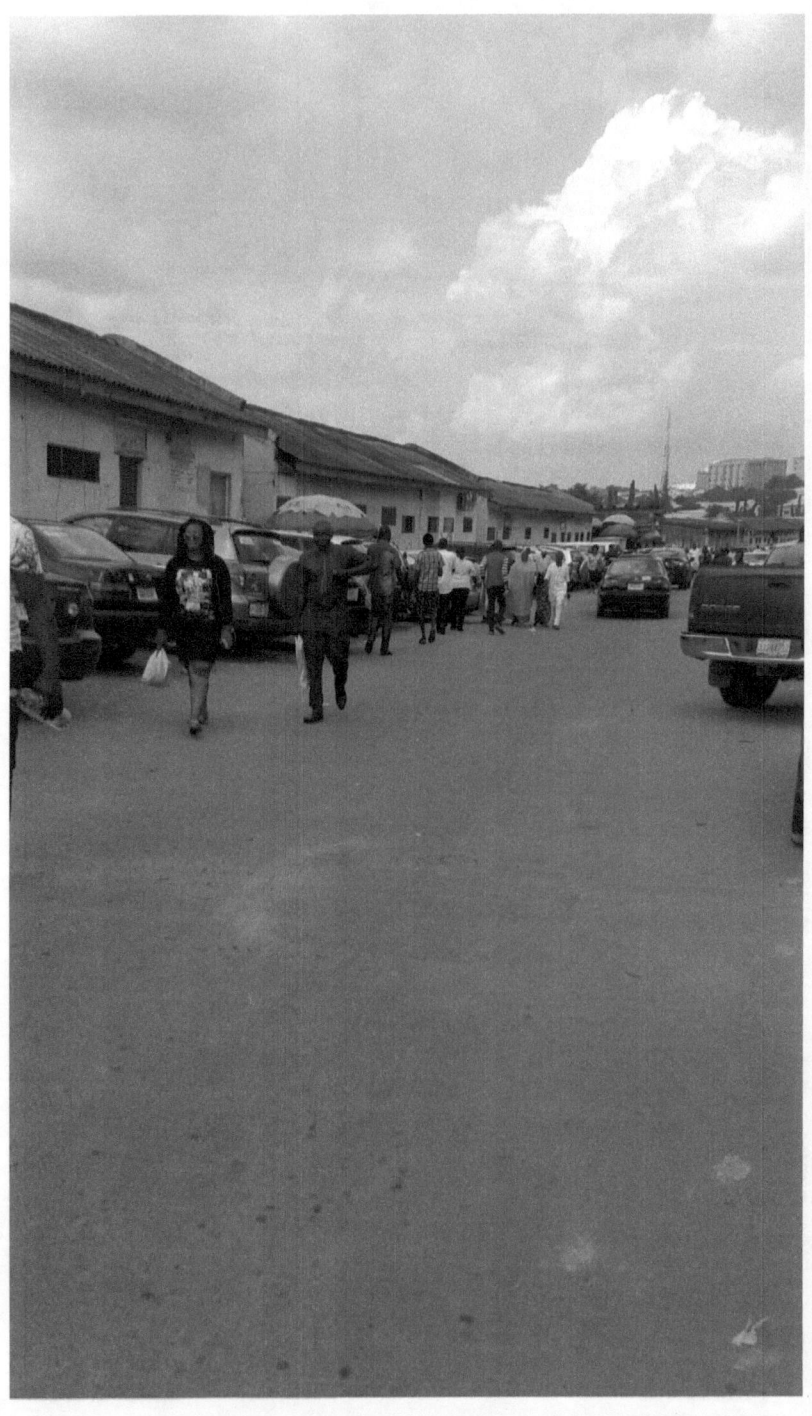

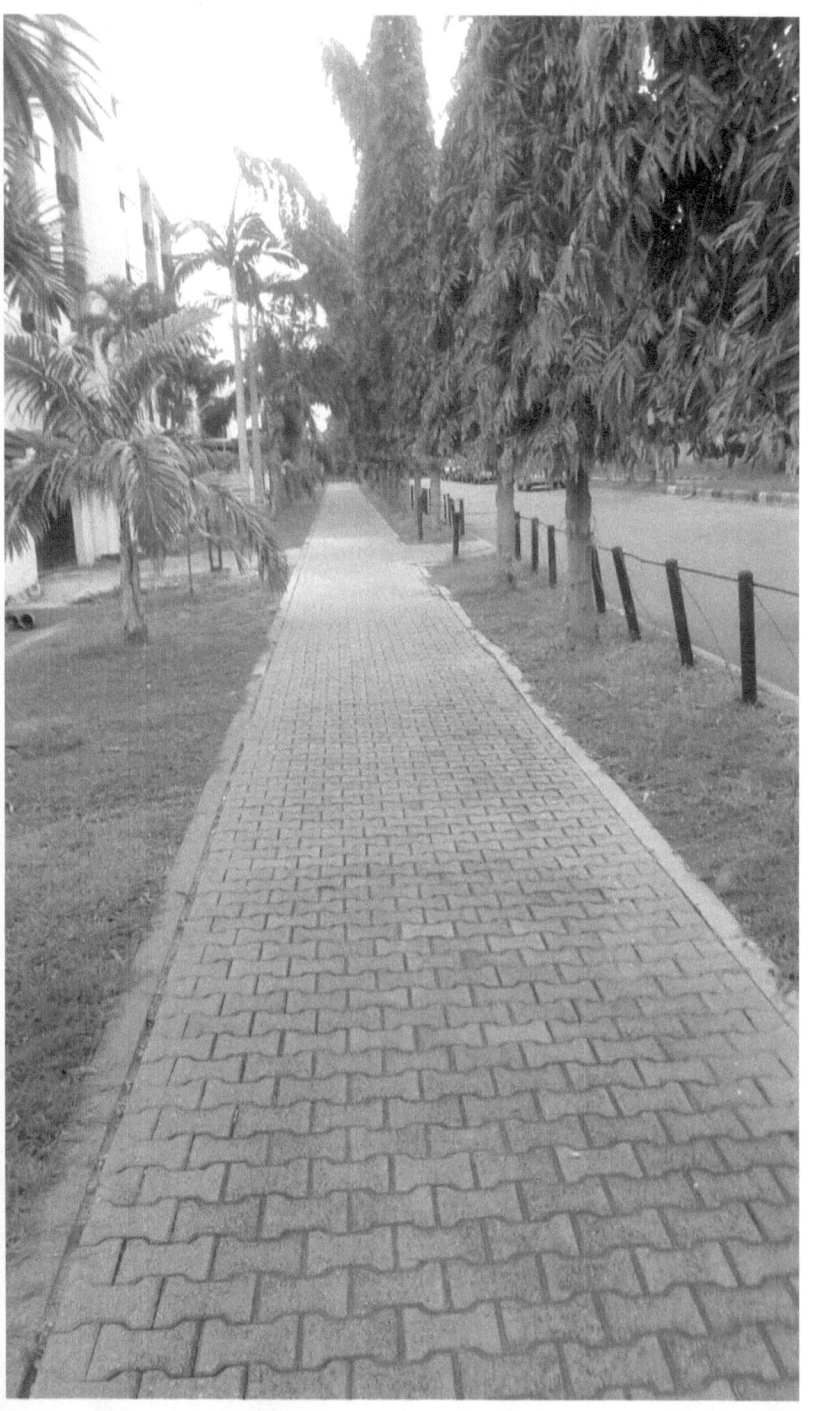

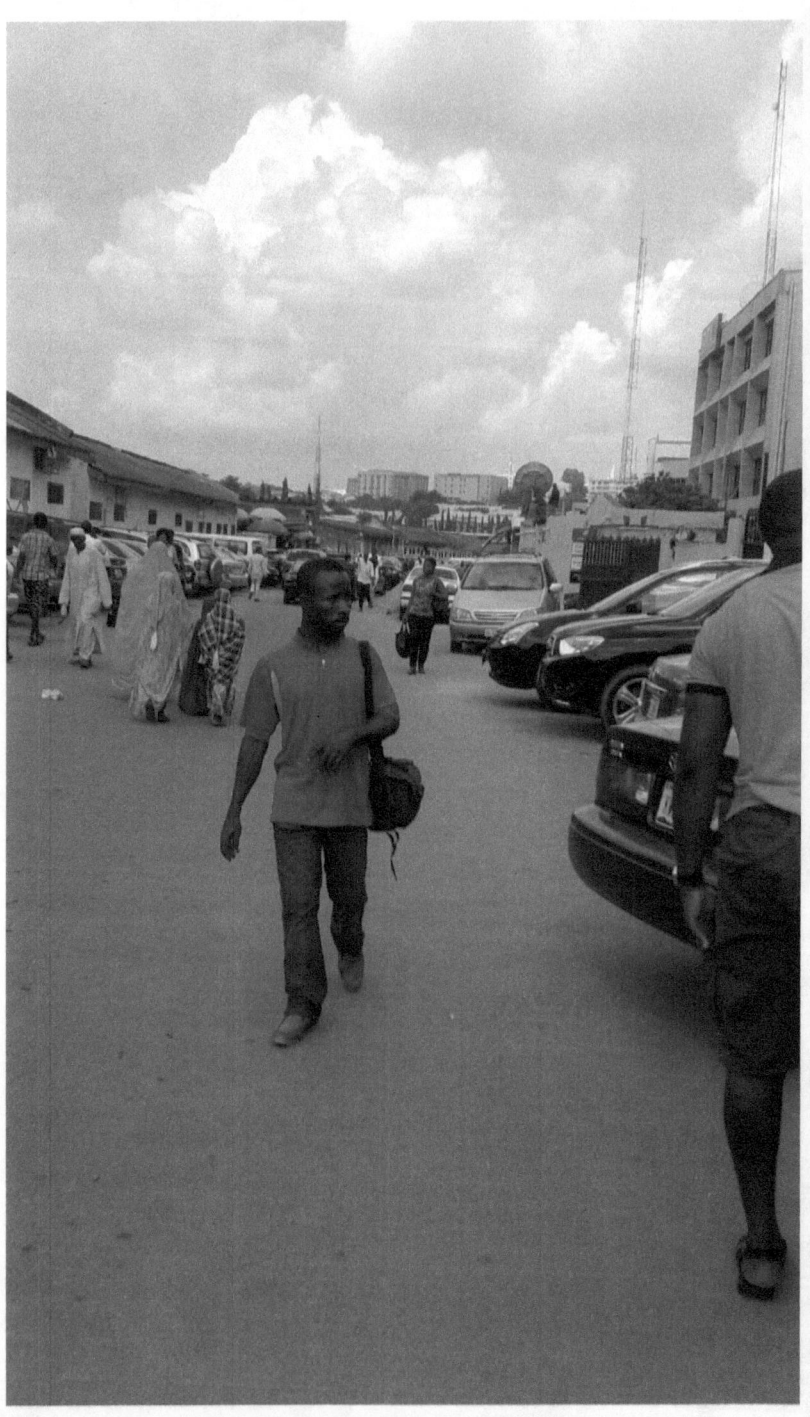

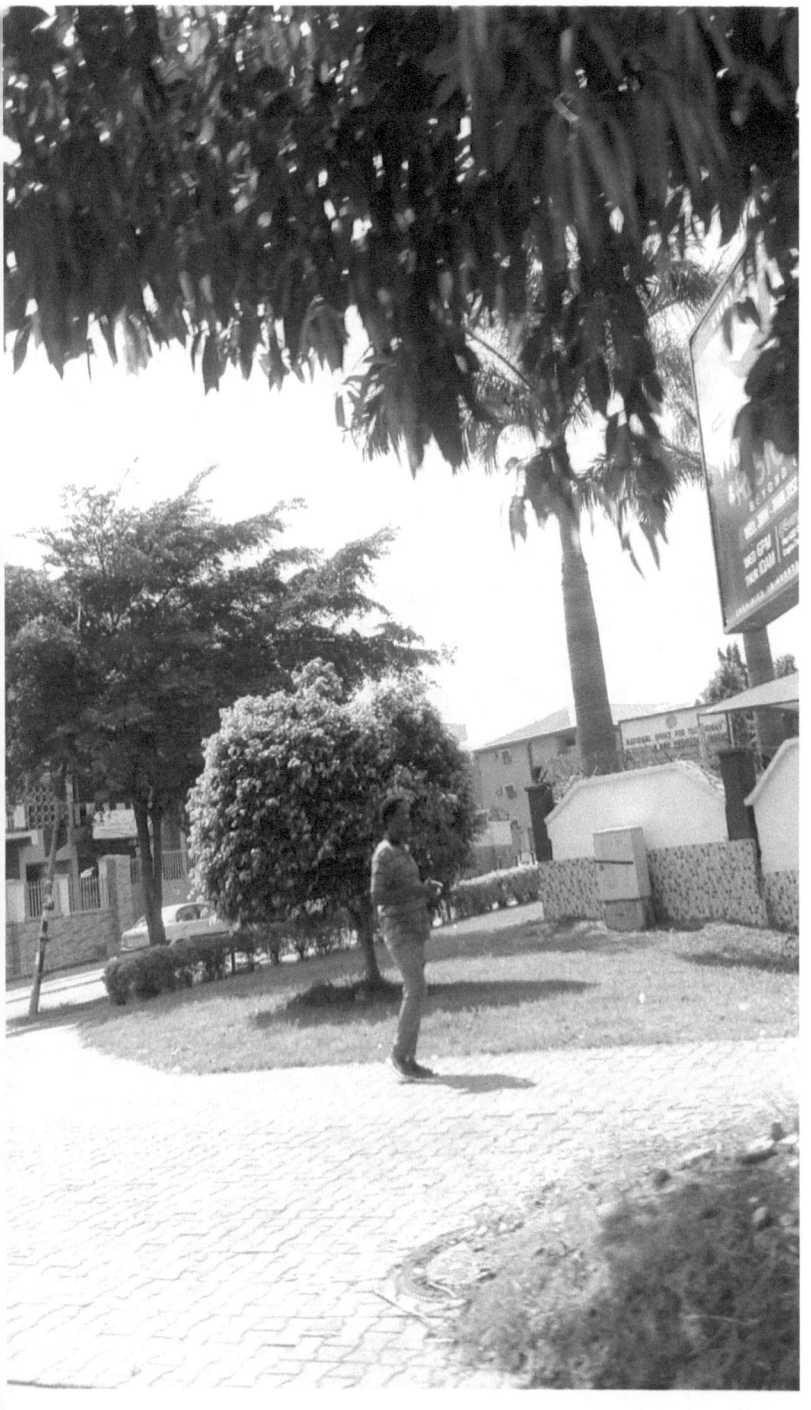

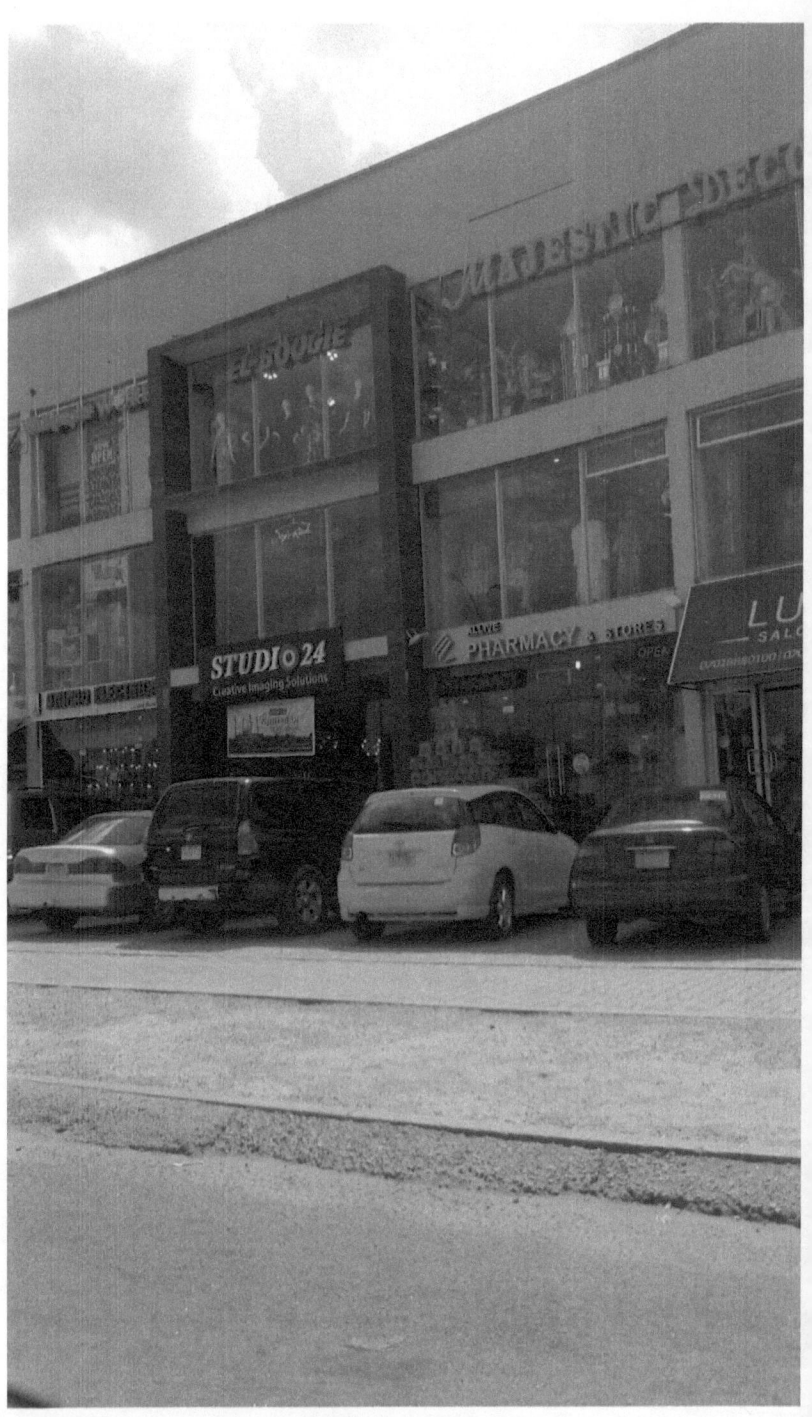

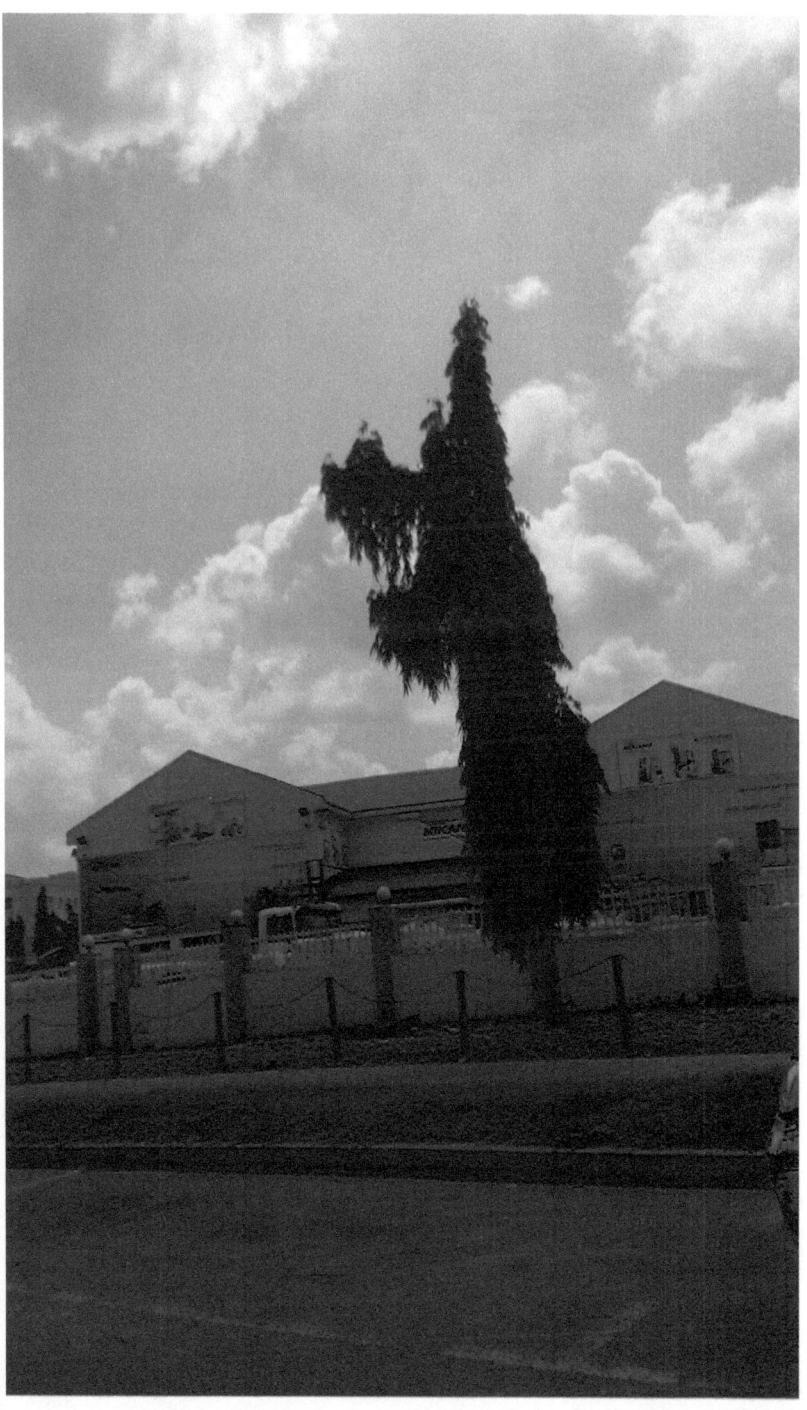

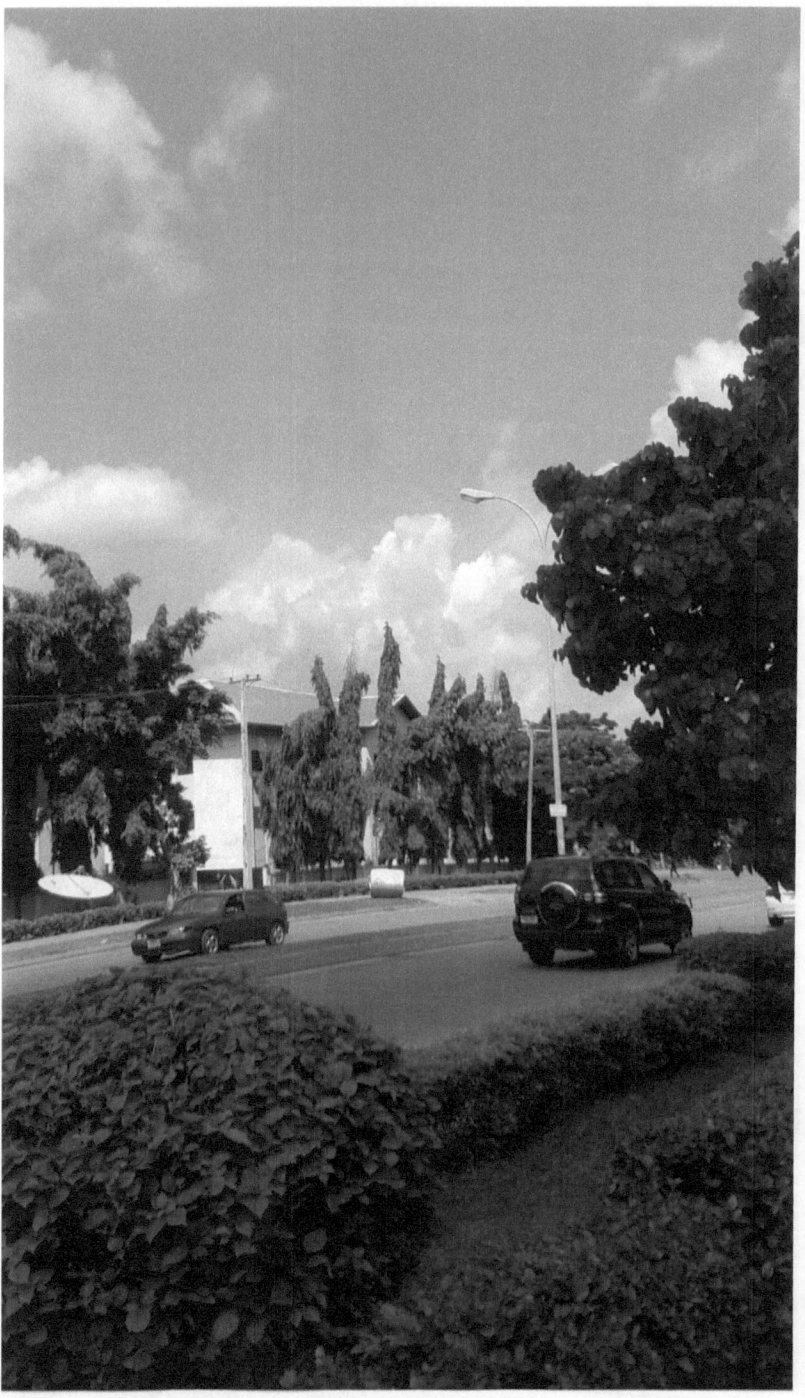

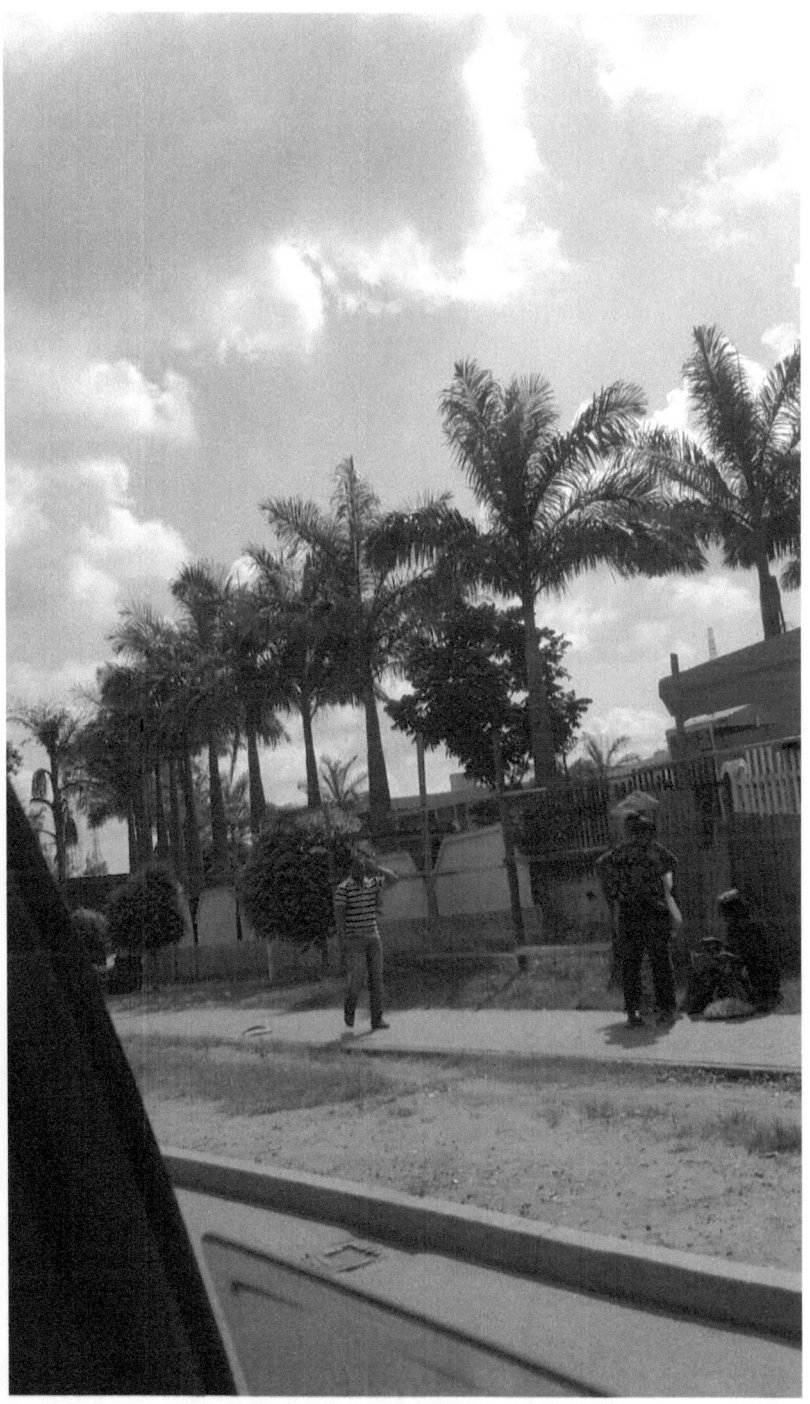

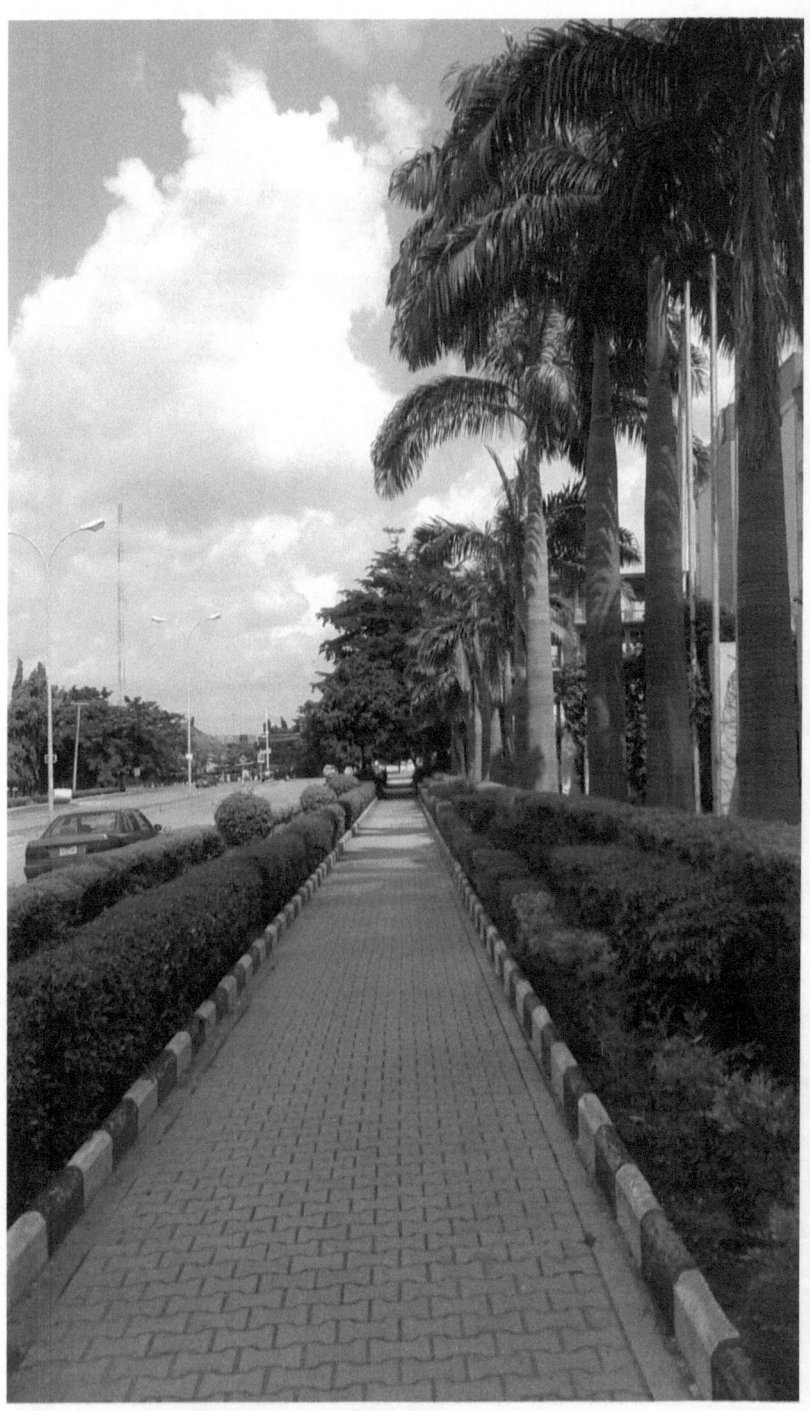

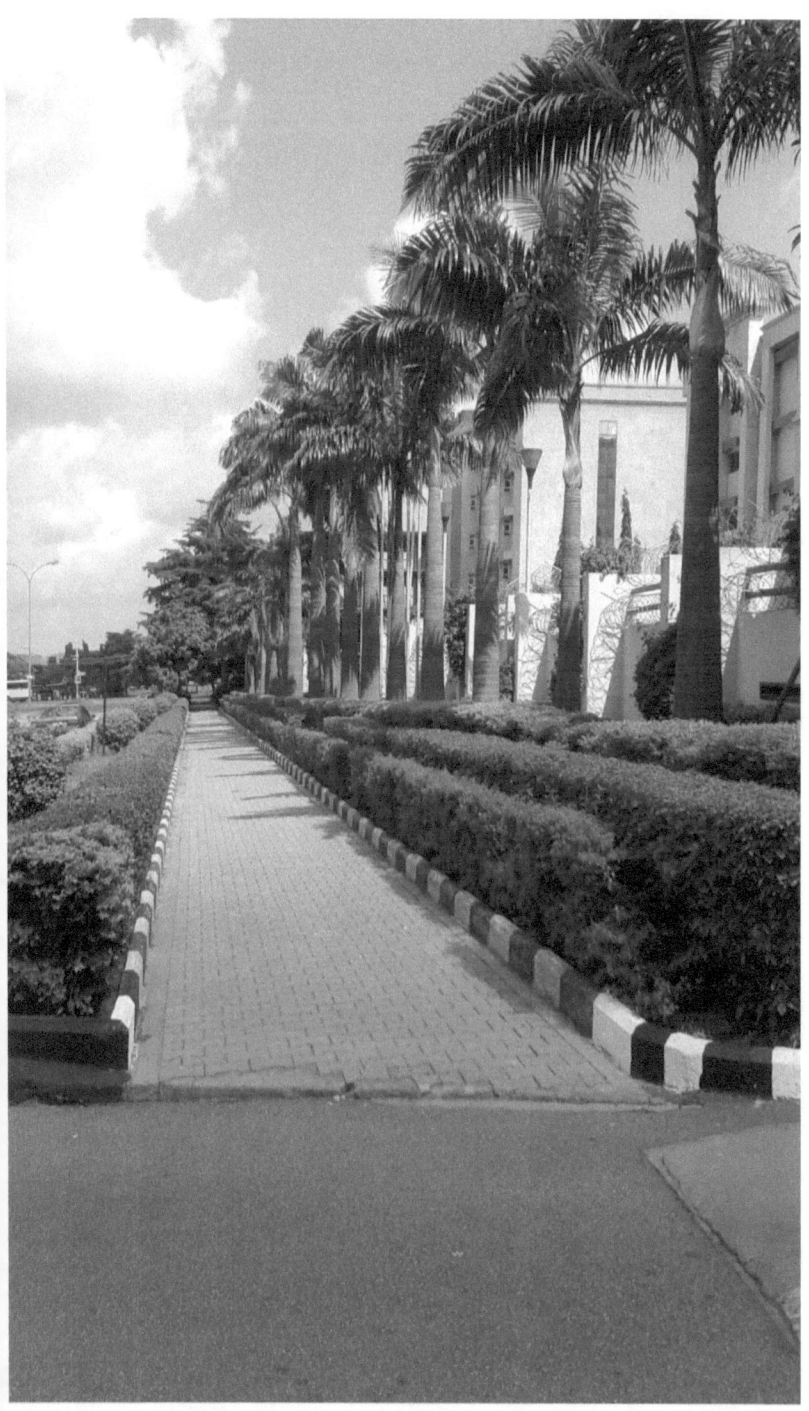

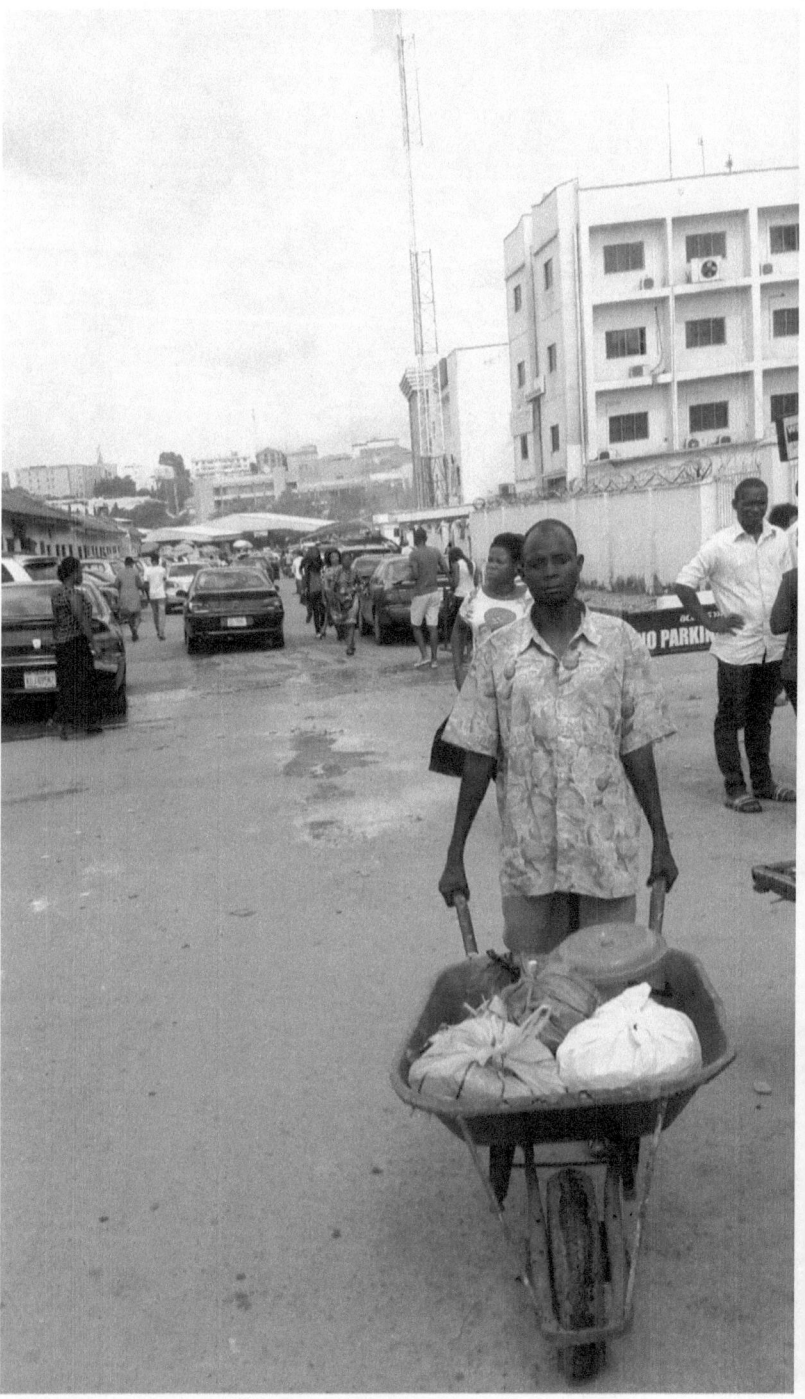

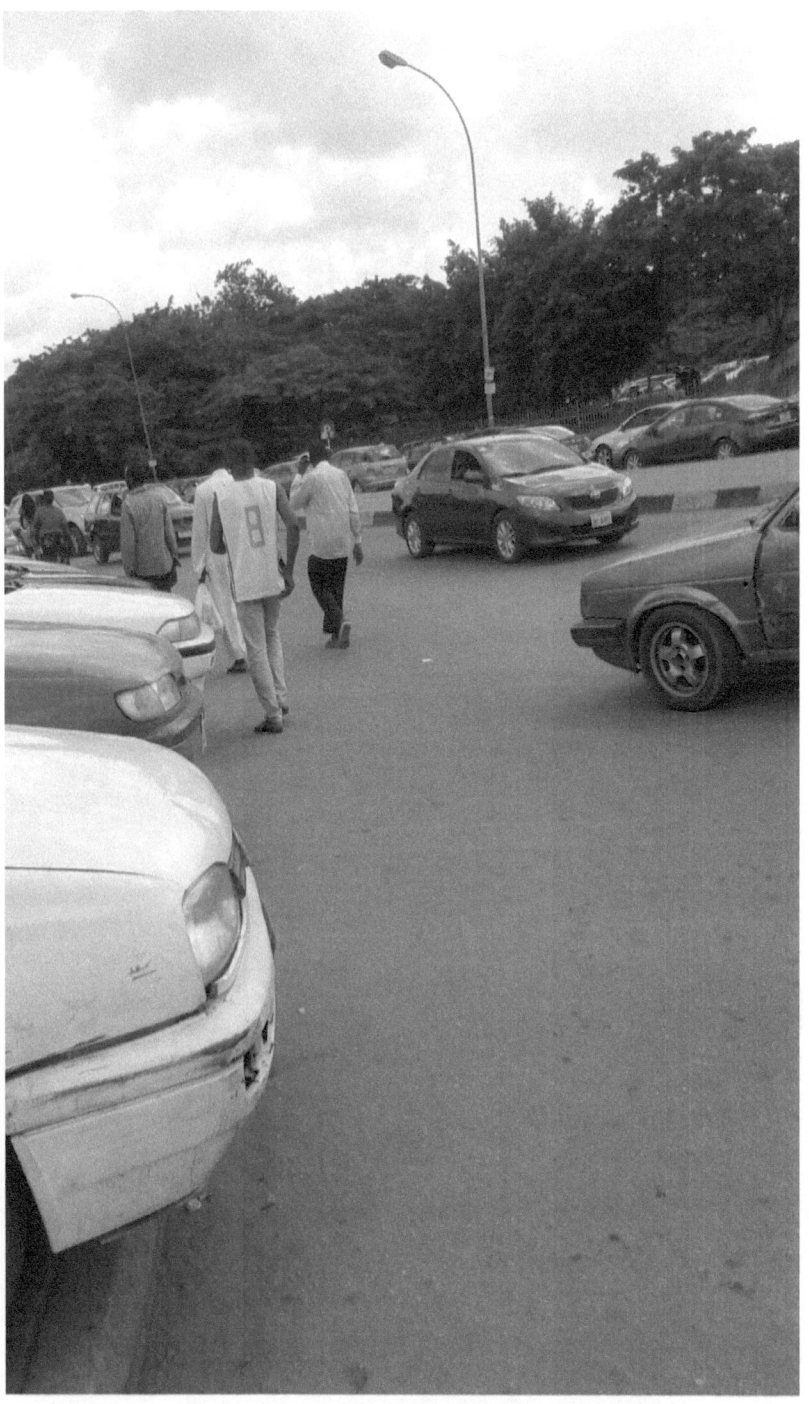

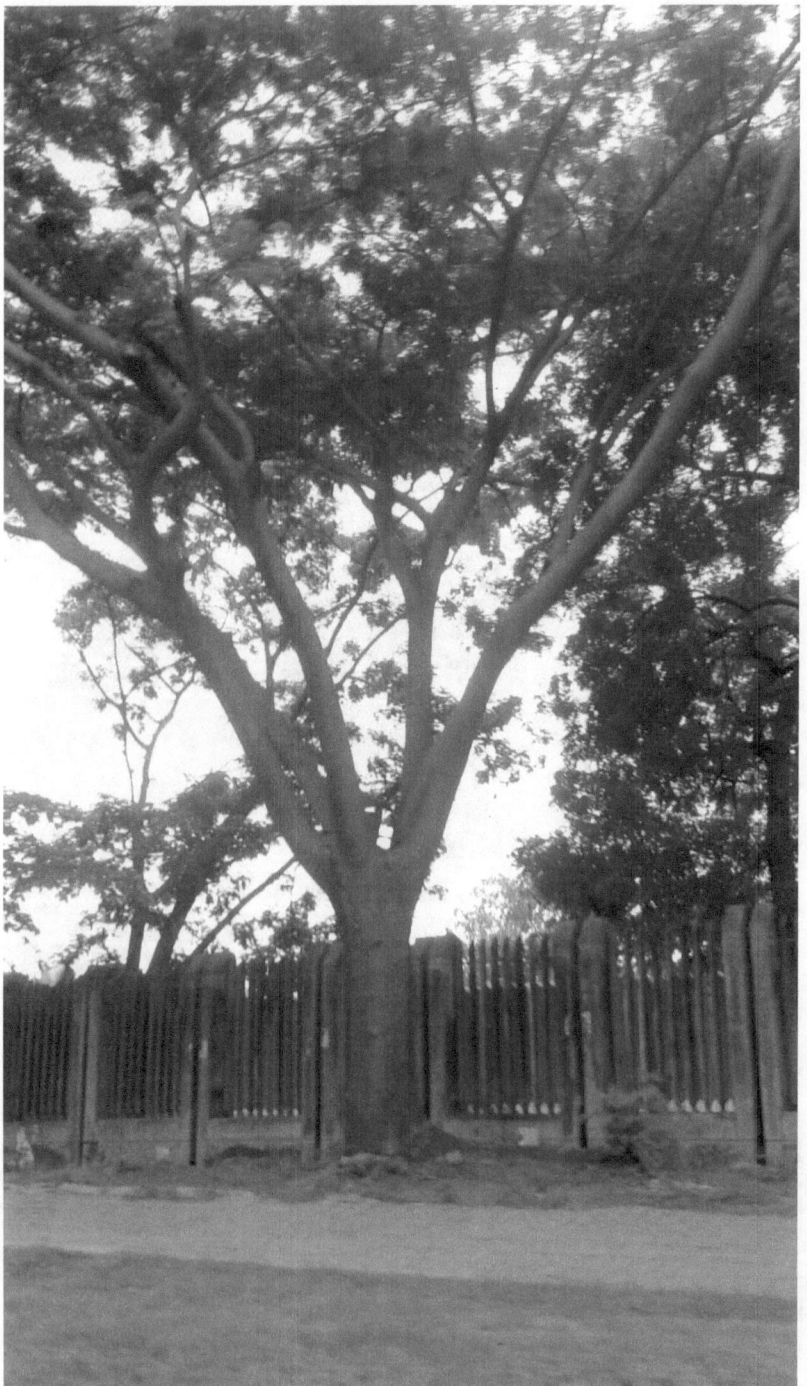

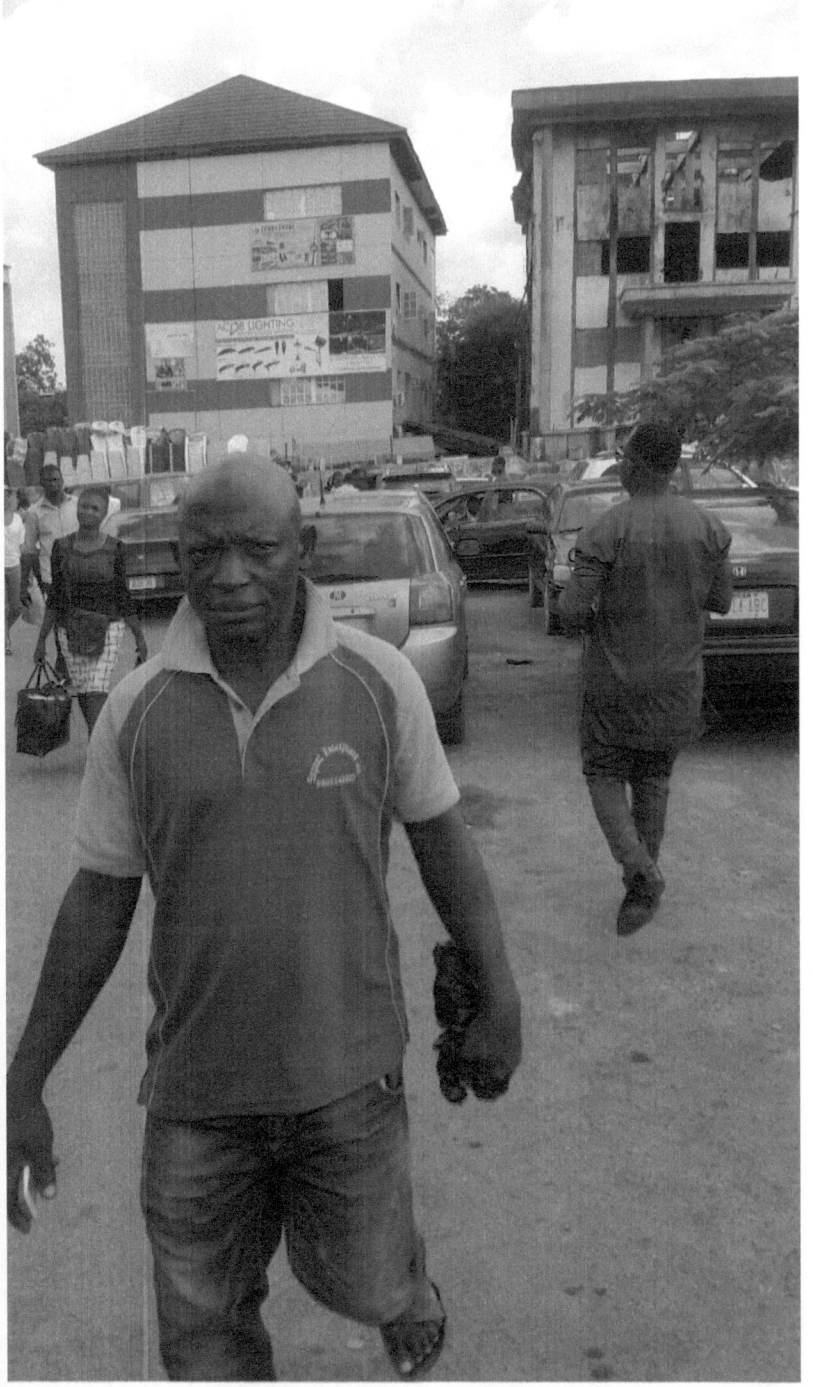

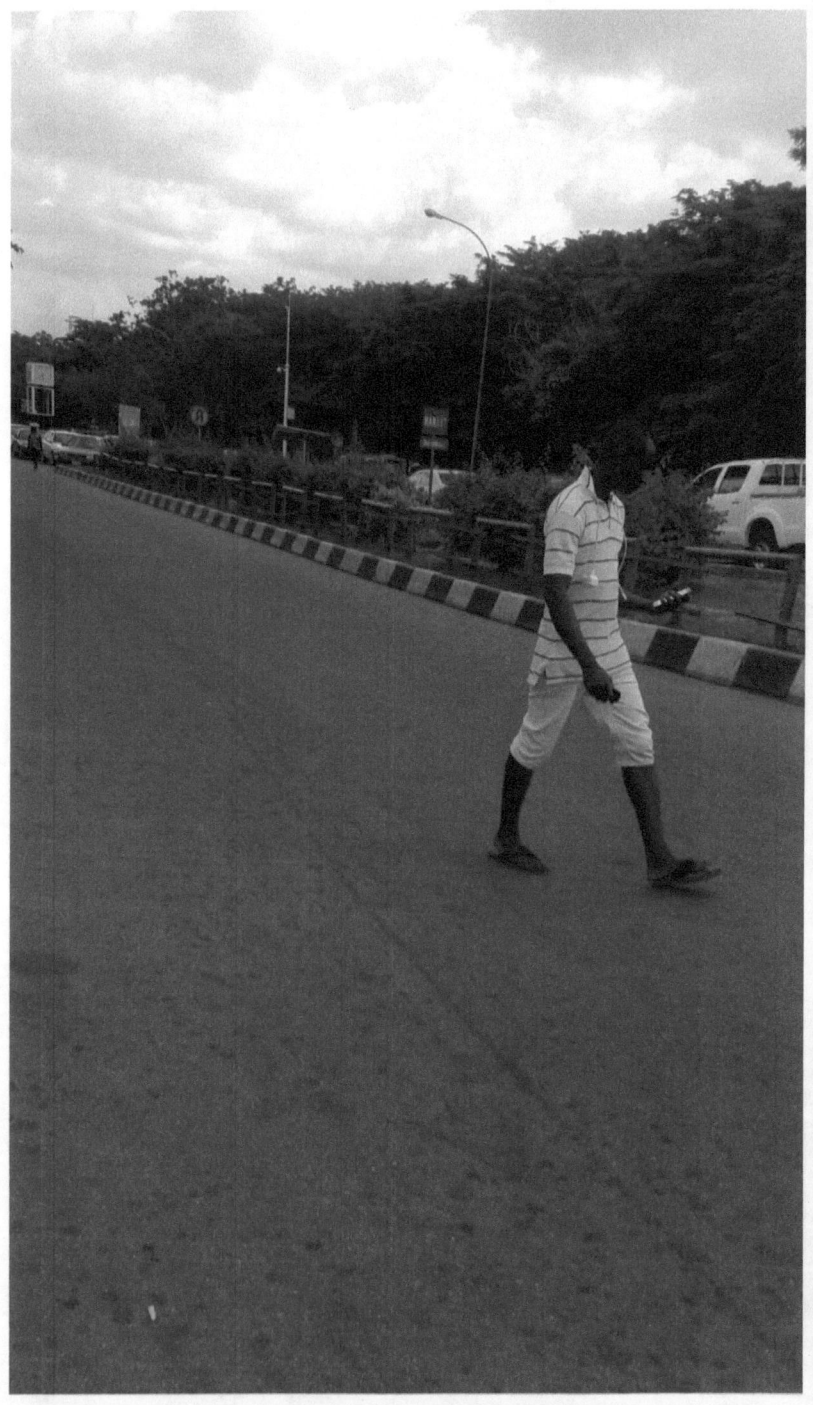